GUIDING PRINCIPLES

GUIDING PRINCIPLES

The Spirit of Our Traditions

World Service Office
PO Box 9999
Van Nuys, CA 91409
TEL (818) 773-9999
FAX (818) 700-0700
WEB www.na.org

World Service Office–CANADA
Mississauga, Ontario

World Service Office–EUROPE
Brussels, Belgium
TEL +32/2/646 6012

World Service Office–IRAN
Tehran, Iran
WEB www.na-iran.org

Printed in China.

18 17 16   5 4 3 2

ISBN 978-1-63380-085-4 (Hardcover)   WSO Catalog Item No. 1201

ISBN 978-1-63380-086-1 (Softcover)   WSO Catalog Item No. 1202

This is NA Fellowship-approved literature.

TABLE OF CONTENTS

INTRODUCTION

Guiding Principles

Our Twelve Traditions are about relationships: with ourselves, our groups, our service bodies, and our Higher Power. While they address our practices in service, they also provide a foundation for us to learn how to live. They are practical and spiritual at the same time. Our Traditions help us to navigate: They remind us where we are going and where we are likely to run aground. They also remind us that we steer our own ship. Unity and autonomy guide us, not uniformity and governance. We surrender authority to a Higher Power and come together as equals. Our primary purpose is to carry the message to the addict who still suffers. If we are to accomplish that, we need recovery ourselves, and we need to come together in unity to build the groups and provide the services that make recovery available to us all. We need every principle, every resource, and every member.

Humility, empathy, and love are keys to selfless service, and selfless service frees us from the self-centeredness at the core of our disease. Yet many of us who have tried to recover on service alone find, sooner or later, that without doing the hard work of the Twelve Steps, we don't have tools to live by these principles. We need the Steps if we are to follow the Traditions— and we need the Traditions to create an atmosphere in which we find the love, safety, and anonymity necessary to work the Steps.

Together, our Steps and Traditions allow us to grow and thrive, to interact with others, and to sustain ourselves through difficulty. These spiritual principles and practices can guide us in our decisions in service and throughout our lives. Although we each have different ways of connecting with and learning about the Traditions, we can all agree that these are the principles that keep us alive and free.

The Twelve Traditions have been part of the spiritual foundation of NA as we know it from our very beginnings. The principles arose out of experience: practical lessons learned from problems faced early in the development of our predecessor, Alcoholics Anonymous. Earlier programs created for addicts, including some bearing the same name, did not practice Traditions and did not survive. Even the NA we know today was nearly lost. Only when some of our founding members insisted on following the Traditions did our Fellowship begin to experience stability and growth. Those early members understood the necessity of the Traditions for our survival. Our need for these principles is just as great today.

Our Traditions make our principles very clear, yet understanding and application will draw us to study, interpretation, and growth. The principles that keep our Fellowship alive and free are universal, allowing us to be incredibly flexible. NA can flourish and thrive in cultures and contexts around the world. The Twelve Traditions are not negotiable, and that means they cannot be bought, bartered, traded on, or sold. That doesn't mean we are rigid, inflexible, or incapable of growth. Rather than seeing our Traditions as limiting, we come to understand that they point the way to freedom. Our guiding principles help us steer clear of pitfalls, allowing us continued growth and change.

Tradition is practice, developed over time, which reflects both belief and identity. Traditions create continuity—they bind people together. Although traditions are vital to any community, the way any given tradition is practiced can evolve. A family may come together for the same holiday meal over the course of many generations, but every year there may be differences in the celebration. The important elements remain stable—we come together in love and unity, as part of something valuable and enduring. Our guiding principles don't change, but the way we practice them grows and develops as we do.

Our principles remain the same, but we face fresh challenges to them all the time. A new problem in one community is often an old problem in another. As in our personal recovery, we often feel unique or alone when we struggle, but most of our struggles are shared. If we are willing to be open about our difficulties and seek experience, mostly we find someone who has been through the same thing. Sometimes, though, we must still go through it to learn for ourselves.

Some experienced members saw this firsthand when they were doing outreach work with newer members in a place where NA was just getting started. One by one, the members from older communities shared their experience with the Twelve Traditions of NA. Some were emotional; some were philosophical; some went deep into the history and origins of these principles. Each time, when the speaker finished, one of the newer members listening would ask a question like "Yeah, okay, but can we buy refreshments for the meeting?"

If all the answers were provided for us, we wouldn't have to spend so much time in discussion. Simple issues wouldn't bring us together or drive us to reach out, and we wouldn't learn much that way. As we build our relationship to our Traditions, questions like "Can we serve refreshments?" can bring us to examine our principles, our values, our priorities, and the ways we make decisions in our groups.

When we allow these discussions the time and energy they deserve, our understanding of the spiritual principles underlying the Twelve Traditions deepens, and so does our practice. There are countless ways we can learn about the Traditions, from simply hearing them read in meetings to studying them in great detail. One member shared that his first learning experience with the Traditions came through a simple exercise: "My first sponsor told me to read the Twelve Traditions aloud to myself, replacing NA with my own name. It felt awkward at first, but it gave me a new way to look at the Traditions." Whatever way our work in the Traditions begins, the learning process is an ongoing journey, much like our work in the Steps.

The chapter "What Can I Do?" from our Basic Text encourages new members to take the steps outlined in the previous chapter as a way of answering the questions that may be troubling us. "Begin your own program by taking Step One from the previous chapter, 'How It Works.' . . . Go on to Step Two, and so forth, and as you go on you will come to an understanding of the program for yourself." This is a critical line in our literature, and its appearance in the chapter that falls between the Twelve Steps and Twelve Traditions is not coincidental. Even as we practice a program of recovery that is outlined for us in our literature and shared with us by our sponsors and in meetings, ultimately we will come to our own understanding. In fact, it is necessary for us to do so, if NA recovery will be a way of life for us and not just a phase we pass through. We must understand and make it our own.

Understanding the Traditions is part of coming to an understanding of the program for ourselves. If "it is only through understanding and application that they work," how do we learn to understand and apply our Traditions? In our groups across the Fellowship and around the world, we've been answering this question for many years. But the answers to particular questions are not always the same. When we are engaged in creative action of the spirit, whether in our personal lives or in our service work, we may be surprised by the solutions that present themselves. This book offers a set of tools that can help each of us to learn about our principles, consider some challenging questions, and come to an understanding for ourselves.

About This Book

This book emerged from a driving need for greater understanding of the principles of our Traditions and how we apply them. Around the world, NA members have sought practical, simple, experience-based material on the Twelve Traditions. There are many differences in the ways we understand and practice these principles within our Fellowship, and this workbook does not presume to declare one way of thinking or practicing right or wrong. At the same time, it wouldn't serve us very well to write a book that didn't help us answer the questions that trouble us so greatly.

We gathered experience, strength, and hope from addicts across our Fellowship: worksheets handed down from sponsor to sponsee; notes from hundreds of workshops; personal writings sent in by members around the world; stacks of speaker recordings. Together the workgroup sorted through this material, finding themes and practices that were common and language that helped us understand in new ways. We counted every word, and we tried to make every word count. The writing exercises, discussion prompts, and workshop questions that follow come from material that members have been creating and using in smaller groups. This book comes from long discussions, sharing, and the many, many questions we ask. Like all of our literature, this book is written by addicts, for addicts, from the shared experience of addicts recovering in Narcotics Anonymous. The result is a collection of tools and experience on how to work through issues together, using the principles embodied in the Traditions.

Working together brings us to common understanding; the conscience of a group develops as the group solves problems and handles routine business.

We think a lot about our Traditions; we argue about them a lot, too. This workbook is not another service manual or an abstract collection of ideas, but a set of tools to help us think about and apply the Traditions without tearing ourselves apart in the process.

As members awaken spiritually and share with one another, their answers get woven into the fabric of the Fellowship's conventional wisdom. Then, just when our thinking begins to harden into dogma, another generation comes along to challenge us and keep our perspective fresh. We remain open-minded and flexible. It is important to look to our literature and our experienced members for guidance, but ultimately each member has the right to understand and apply this program in the way that works best. It is our hope that this book will provide something for everyone on this path, although some parts of it might be more useful for some of us than for others. We invite you to take what you need and leave the rest.

In This Book

The Traditions are a set of guiding principles for working together, and the tools, text, and questions here are meant to facilitate discussion and inspire action in our groups, in workshops, and in sponsorship. The material in this workbook is divided into sections for individuals, groups, and service bodies. It may be that an individual member finds useful material in the group section, or that a service body comes to life around a question directed at an individual. The structure is modular—it can be used in any combination. This workbook doesn't need to be read or worked from beginning to end.

When we keep an open mind, even casual conversation can transform our understanding. "I had an H&I commitment about an hour from where I lived," shared a member. "There'd be three or four of us in the car and we'd talk about the program the whole way there and back. I learned more about our Traditions in that car than anywhere else." Sharing our experience, exploring ideas together, thinking about our principles, and making decisions all contribute to our ever-evolving understanding. Staying open-minded and teachable about our basic principles allows our understanding to deepen and mature. We don't ever have to finish learning—even about the things we know best.

The questions in this book are not meant to be a complete and final list; we hope that they will start conversations more than they finish them. It's our belief that a member, group, or service body coming to the project of studying Traditions probably has a pretty clear idea of its questions already. We hope that the questions here will spark discussion and thought, that they will bring you to read, write, and consider—and that at least some of the time, it will be clear that for all but our most fundamental questions there's usually more than one right answer.

Coming to shared understanding is different from telling each other what the rules are. We would be selling ourselves short if we suggested that application of these principles were a simple matter of not breaking rules. If Narcotics Anonymous were a program of compliance, most of us would have walked away—or would have been asked to leave. As with the Twelve Steps, we learn about these principles through experience.

In the chapters that follow, there are many pieces and parts, designed to work together or separately. Each Tradition begins with readings and exercises for all, followed by sections for members, groups, and service bodies. These are meant as a guide for writing or discussion, as topics for group inventory or a group business meeting, and as prompts for discussion in a service workshop. The descriptions that follow are meant to help serve as a guide through the parts of each chapter. Probably the best instructions for using the information in this workbook, however, are simply to be creative and work with other NA members in the process of learning about the Traditions. Each of us is free to explore this material on our own, of course, in whatever way makes sense. But as with *The NA Step Working Guides*, doing the work is part of a process we take on with our sponsor, our group, and our fellow members.

OPENING AND CLOSING READINGS

Each Tradition begins and ends with a short reading. The first reading offers a reflection on the Tradition in terms of our experience and our program. The closing reading brings together some common ideas and principles from the chapter. These readings frame the work in between, offering perspectives on the Traditions that can help guide our work on our own recovery and in service. They may serve as meditations, or as openings into a larger discussion. They may also be useful as readings in a recovery meeting, in a service committee meeting, or at a workshop.

WORD BY WORD AND SPIRITUAL PRINCIPLES

Two exercises that appear in each chapter stand on their own, as they can be useful for members, in groups, and in service bodies. *Word by Word* prompts us to look at the words and phrases from each Tradition to help build a more complete understanding of the Tradition as a whole. *Spiritual Principles* asks us to do similar work with spiritual principles connected to each Tradition. An example is provided in each of these sections for each Tradition, but there is room for continued exploration, individually or as a group. Some of us use a dictionary to help in this work. As with so many aspects of NA recovery and service, the possibilities for discussion and exploration are endless.

FOR MEMBERS

The sections for members include shared experience and questions for exploration. One member explained that work on the Traditions allowed her to learn "who I am, who I want to be, and how I interact with others." This work can build on and extend our work in the Steps–so it might make sense for us to approach this work in much the same way we do our Step work. For many of us, that includes writing, discussion, meditation, thought, and practice. We might address these questions in writing to share with our sponsor, or use them to guide a conversation. We may also find that these questions lead to other questions, or that our discussion takes us into new territory. Sharing with our sponsor, trusted NA friends, or fellow servants is an important part of this work.

FOR GROUPS

The section for our groups within each chapter offers experience, strength, and hope for NA groups seeking to understand and apply the Traditions more effectively. Again, the section opens with some shared experience followed by questions for group inventory. Some groups may choose to answer one or two questions each month, or to schedule workshops before or after a meeting. Some groups may choose to conduct an annual inventory on all Twelve Traditions, while others might want to work through one Tradition at a time. Our hope is simply that this material helps groups to be successful in their efforts to carry the NA message to the addict who still suffers.

IN SERVICE

Whenever we come together in service, we are already practicing the Traditions. Discussing a Tradition together helps us to build a common bond. We don't all need to agree on how to understand or apply a Tradition, but we can come to appreciate our different perspectives and understand our differing points of view. Our various understandings can enrich our culture of service, rather than serve as sources of conflict or division. The sections for service bodies help us to explore the Traditions we are practicing. The text and questions included in the service section of each chapter offer a variety of approaches for coming together to discuss the Traditions in a spirit of unity and cooperation.

GROUP INVENTORY AND SERVICE WORKSHOPS

The text and questions in the group and service sections of each Tradition are meant to help NA groups and service bodies discuss our guiding principles. Each group and service committee is free to discuss these sections and questions in a way that makes the most sense based on their needs and resources. The discussion questions that are included in these chapters are simply meant to serve as conversation starters. The most important part of any of these discussions will be the sharing of experience and perspectives that happens within each group, service body, or workshop. For this reason, it may be most effective to choose just one or two questions for any given group inventory meeting or workshop. Those who are helping to organize a discussion may wish to choose a question or two in advance—asking those who are participating to help in the selection, if possible—and encourage those participating to read the section from the Tradition prior to the discussion. The section might also be read before introducing the question to be discussed. As with so much else that happens in NA, the free exchange of experience and ideas in an atmosphere of support and mutual respect leads to growth and understanding. The Traditions are our guiding principles, and as our reading reminds us, "it is only through understanding and application that they work."

There is no one right way to use this book. The wrong way to use this book is as some kind of qualifier or proof of "having worked the Traditions properly." We do ourselves a disservice when we create new requirements for membership or service, or when we suggest that one addict's recovery or contribution in service is more legitimate than another's.

This book won't tell you whether to serve refreshments in your home group, but we hope it will make it easier for your group to come to decisions it can grow with. And we hope that each of us will find a deeper relationship to these principles in our NA service, in our spirituality, and in our own lives.

Our common welfare should come first; personal recovery depends on NA unity.

TRADITION

Unity changes us. When we rise above our differences we start to understand who we are, how we fit, and how much we have to offer the world. The degradation of addiction robs us of self-respect. The care and respect we show each other in Narcotics Anonymous reminds us of our own value and humanity. The experience of unity restores us to dignity.

Our willingness to come together in unity and anonymity means we recognize that each of us matters. The Basic Text tells us in Step Eight, "We want to look the world in the eye with neither aggressiveness nor fear." Then, in Chapter Nine, the Basic Text mentions, "We no longer need to make fools of ourselves by standing up for nonexistent virtues." These passages describe freedom from animosity. When we feel dignity, we are not turned by a passing breeze, and we no longer need to defend ourselves from every shadow.

We often say "our unity is our strength," and it's true for us both as individuals and as a Fellowship: We draw personal strength from NA unity. We know that today we don't have to go it alone. We walk together on this path, and the addict yet to come will follow in our footsteps. We draw strength, courage, and honor from being part of something so much greater than ourselves.

NA unity is our bond with fellow addicts:
those who came before us, those who are
here today, and those who have yet to find us.
Our practice of unity makes room for
all addicts to recover in NA.

Tradition One

Our commitment to unity is essential in Narcotics Anonymous. Anonymity is our spiritual foundation; unity is the practical framework that binds us together. We need each other, every one of us. Unity is an active force and a principle we practice. In unity we find a safe place to surrender, and the ability to carry our Higher Power's will beyond our wildest dreams.

Unity is the key to our survival and the beginning of our miracle. Practicing unity can be as simple as a smile—but it can also be one of the most difficult things we do. For the alienated, frightened, and resentful people many of us were when we got here, "our common welfare" can be hard to imagine. Our personal recovery depends on a principle we may never have experienced. Practicing unity is an act of faith.

Putting our common welfare first gives us a way out of the self-obsession at the core of our disease. When we think of ourselves less and our fellows more, we contribute to NA unity. We set aside differences to help a newcomer. Friendships survive disagreements and grow stronger. We start to trust that NA is strong enough to hold us.

We can be so afraid of getting it wrong that we hesitate to take any risks at all. That fear can undermine us in our lives, our groups, and our efforts to carry the message. Recovery sometimes means making new mistakes instead of repeating old ones. There is no way to avoid growing pains. While we always strive to do the right thing, our most powerful lessons can come through our mistakes—if we are open to learning from them.

The description of our symbol in the Basic Text explains that the outer circle represents a universal program "that has room within it for all manifestations of the recovering person." Narcotics Anonymous offers hope to addicts around the world, regardless of any real or imagined differences that might separate us. It can be easier to feel unity with addicts in faraway places than with the people we know and serve with. Unity is not just a feeling; it's a decision that shapes our actions and our attitudes.

WORD BY WORD

Define, expand on, or clarify the words or phrases from this Tradition, one at a time or in relation to each other, for writing or discussion with your sponsor or other NA members.

Example: welfare

Welfare is a word that's used more than it's understood. *Welfare* typically refers to our health, comfort, and well-being. Many definitions of this word also mention safety and happiness. When Tradition One suggests that our common welfare should come first, it's telling us that the well-being of the group should be more important than the desires of the individual. Together, as a Fellowship, we all share a common responsibility for each other and for the Fellowship that makes our personal recovery possible.

SPIRITUAL PRINCIPLES

Each Tradition embodies a variety of spiritual principles. The list of principles and values below may be useful as we consider applications of this Tradition. Explore them in writing or discussion with your sponsor or other NA members. If other principles or values not listed below seem relevant for you, include those as well.

- unity
- selflessness
- hospitality
- surrender
- love
- empathy
- acceptance
- anonymity
- goodwill
- commitment
- safety

Example: unity

When we experience unity with the group, we call it commitment. When we experience unity within ourselves, we call it integrity. Of course, this doesn't come automatically. Each example of unity begins with surrender. Personal recovery begins with surrender to the First Step; surrender to the First Tradition brings us to understand that we are part of something much greater than ourselves.

The atmosphere of recovery that helps us welcome newcomers is made possible through unity. When we are in conflict with each other, when a meeting is full of tension or bitterness, it doesn't matter what we say: A message of hope won't get through. On the other hand, unity is a message in itself. When we walk into our first meeting and see addicts coming together in unity, the spirit touches us even before the words get through.

For Members

Tradition One asks us to shift our perspective. For the first time, "we" comes before "me." That commitment is the beginning of new freedom. We learn to let go. We start to see that the group can be trusted to make decisions. There is a bridge to Tradition One from Step Twelve: Love and service are principles of each. When we practice these principles in all our affairs, unity— or the desire for unity—is a natural result. The community must be healthy for us to thrive, but we can't manage or control it into well-being. Addicts learn through example and empathy. A healthy NA community has room for members at all different places in the journey.

The work of the Twelve Steps is necessary to get our mess out of the way and clear a path to our heart. But we can't wait until we finish the Steps to start understanding the Traditions. In so many ways, our relationship to the Traditions begins the first time we walk through the door. The atmosphere of a meeting can carry a more powerful message than the words that are shared. Listening for a Higher Power working through each of us gives us access to solutions none of us had when we walked in the room. When we come together in unity we are open to each other and to the wisdom of a Power greater than ourselves.

Coming to terms with the First Tradition can be challenging. We need each other desperately, and yet we are afraid. This reservation often comes from our experiences of being hurt. We tend to react in dis-unifying ways to the possibility of being hurt again. Our instinct is to meet disease with disease, but when we meet it with love and compassion instead, we create an opportunity for recovery. Addiction separates us from others, and unity is an antidote to alienation. As our trust in the Fellowship grows, we can be less afraid. Unity of purpose keeps us together when feelings are pushing us toward the door. Staying through difficulty is a profound act of surrender. We need each other more than we need our old beliefs.

Unity is our first glimpse out of self-obsession. It begins with the willingness to be honest, and teaches us to listen with an open mind and an open heart to those around us. We can be genuinely pleased to see a former enemy seeking a new way of life in recovery, and even more amazed when that person helps us through a difficult situation. We feel immense joy at seeing an addict begin to recover. One of the purest expressions of goodwill in NA is our heartfelt desire for the newcomer to have freedom. Sometimes it's more genuine than our hope for ourselves. When that desire takes hold, we feel compelled to clear away any distractions between the newcomer and the message.

Practicing these principles can lead us to a desire to learn more about other kinds of spiritual practice as well. Our history has many lessons, and research or study might be part of how we come to understand the Traditions. But practicing the Traditions requires that we understand them with the heart as well as the mind. We learn most about our principles by practicing conscious contact and open-mindedness. Our growing awareness is a source of wisdom. When we are rigid and closed-minded, we can miss the miracle because it doesn't look like we imagine it should. It can be easy to forget how we got where we are today, both as individuals and as groups. Gratitude and a sense of wonder change our perception. Keeping the basics alive is one of the rewards of carrying the message.

The gifts of service far outweigh the work. One member described how service helped make unity a reality for him: "At the end of my first meeting, I was standing around not really knowing what to do or if I wanted to come back. A woman asked if I was new. When I said yes, she welcomed me and then asked if I would empty the trash for the group. I came back every week and emptied the trash. I've been an NA member ever since." Being asked to serve helps us feel useful and visible to other members. It's easier to stay around when we feel useful.

Participation is essential to unity, and it's also how we start to feel like we belong. We talk a lot about service as a responsibility, but it is also a tool. Serving in Narcotics Anonymous helps us to internalize the First Tradition. It teaches us how to live and work with others and how to carry out our Higher Power's will, and often it drives us to the Steps. Freedom from active addiction comes long before we are free from the fear, anger, and regret that compelled us. Learning to act in a spirit of love and unity breaks us out of those old cages.

Caring for our common welfare begins in service, but gradually affects all areas of our lives. Our relationship to this Tradition shows in our behavior and translates directly into our lives outside of NA. In service, communication is necessary for unity, and the same is true in our personal relationships. Learning to communicate effectively is one of the greatest gifts of involvement in NA service; it improves our ability to carry the message, but it also changes our lives at work, at home, and in our daily interactions with others. Good communication is a result of unity, and a necessary condition for it. If we fail to communicate in our marriage, for example, we may soon find it difficult to remain married. When we consider the common welfare of our household, we can set aside immediate desires for the good of all. Surrender allows us to make peace with reality even when it's not going our way. When unity is our guiding principle, there are some arguments we just don't need to have. We can live with differences because we trust the integrity of the bond.

QUESTIONS FOR MEMBERS

The questions below offer a way to begin—or continue—the process of writing, reflection, and discussion of this Tradition with your sponsor or other NA members.

IN NA

1. What does NA unity mean to me? How does my personal recovery depend on it?

2. Do my actions match my beliefs about unity? How do I contribute to unity or disunity?

3. How does anonymity contribute to unity? How does practicing unity help me to place principles before personalities?

4. What additional actions might I take to foster unity in personal recovery, in service, and in social settings?

5. How do I place our common welfare first? How do I demonstrate a commitment to this? Where do I have room to grow?

6. What are my responsibilities as a member of Narcotics Anonymous? Do those responsibilities change over time?

7. How do I show my gratitude? Have I reached out to another addict today?

8. How can I sense when my heart is open or closed to newcomers? What can I do better to help still-suffering addicts?

9. Do my opinions about fellow members separate me—or them—from the group?

10. How am I of service to NA? What types of service work am I most comfortable doing? What service would I like to take on?

11. How does this Tradition help me understand anonymity? How does anonymity help me understand this Tradition? How do I practice anonymity in terms of this Tradition?

12. Describe any bridges between this Tradition and one or more of the Twelve Steps. What do these bridges teach me about my recovery?

13. What more can I do to put the principles of this Tradition into action? How would applying this Tradition change my attitudes and actions?

IN ALL OUR AFFAIRS

14. How have I applied this Tradition outside NA? How else might the principles of this Tradition guide my thinking or my actions?

15. Outside of NA, what are some places where I share common welfare with others? At work, with family, in my local or spiritual community? Where else? List those relationships and describe. How can or do I place common welfare first?

16. How does feeling accepted influence my attitudes and actions?

17. How does practicing acceptance and tolerance affect my attitudes and actions?

18. How can I seek unity in my relationships? What would change about my attitude, my actions, my beliefs?

19. In what other areas of my life might this Tradition be useful? What other opportunities are there for me to seek unity?

For Groups

NA is a program of attraction, and unity is attractive. We feel unity in a group when we see members reaching out and sharing with goodwill. We receive the love of the group in the spirit in which it's given, even if we haven't experienced love before. We hear the message and begin to understand we are not unique, and we are not alone. Feeling like we belong gives us hope. Love and humility in the group inspires freedom and security in the group's members.

The group is the heart of Narcotics Anonymous. Groups hold recovery meetings and guide our service efforts. In NA groups we hear the message, carry the message, create an atmosphere of recovery, and find a home. Serving, sharing, praying, and playing together, our relationships with fellow addicts become intimate and important to us. A home group is not the only place we attend meetings or the only place we express our membership in NA. But it's a place where we attend meetings regularly, take responsibility for the well-being of the group, find our voice, and make sure the door is open.

When the group has an understanding of our Traditions and members are clear and focused, the message shines through. A clear NA message is a source and a reflection of unity. NA language is not a dress code or a requirement for membership, but clarity helps everyone to understand the message of Narcotics Anonymous. We use distinct language in NA, but we cannot expect people to know or understand this language when they first walk in the door. Being scolded or lectured rarely feels welcoming or helpful. The ability to say clearly and simply what we mean is the result of understanding. When we are helping others learn how to share, reinforcement is more powerful than enforcement. It demonstrates that we are listening, not just looking for an angle or an argument. When our divisions get the best of us, the message is lost, even if we say all the right words. We need all the tools we have to foster unity: our Steps, Traditions, and Concepts as well as empathy, patience, and courage.

One of the most important things we do in NA is to listen. For most of us, the experience of sharing and really being heard sets NA apart from anything we've experienced before. When we share in a meeting and the room is quiet, attentive, and present to us—that's a priceless gift. When we realize that speaking the truth is useful, we start to develop a sense of purpose and value. Empathy allows us to recognize our place in the world.

In business meetings, too, listening is vital. Finding common ground takes talking and time. Some of us are more articulate than others. We work hard to hear each other and to help each other express ideas. We show patience, encouragement, and gratitude to our fellows for their involvement, and remember that no voice is greater than any other. We never know where answers will come from or what new solution we might find together. Even disagreements and personal conflicts can serve as the basis for greater unity down the road.

Service helps us feel like we belong. We have a place and a purpose. The experience can be humbling. Doing as the group asks, rather than as we choose, is a form of surrender. When it just plain feels like defeat, surrender requires a deeper trust. We act on faith that a Higher Power is still in charge, and that the greater good will prevail.

Consistency and continuity are vital to our survival, but without rotation, we can risk being frozen in time. When one or a few members dominate a group, it can be hard for others to find a way in. Domination and intimidation stifle the spirit of a group. There is a necessary give-and-take between the oldtimer, the newcomer, and the unseen. It is important to allow new thinking and new ideas into the groups in order to expand our understanding and our ability to reach out.

Each of us shares responsibility for our Fellowship. When we take responsibility, NA starts to feel like it belongs to us. "I was staying at a shelter, and I went to this daytime meeting. The addicts there gave me the opportunity to make coffee. I didn't have a house key or a car key, but I had the NA key. I'd get there early and set it up so perfect, and when I did that I noticed I felt less like harming myself."

One of the most important ways we demonstrate unity is through consistency. We keep our commitments, and that matters to the people around us. Meetings are reliable; they start and end on time. Services continue when trusted servants change. When there is disruption, feelings can spiral out of control quickly. Inconsistency feels like disunity, and often contributes to it. Remembering that unity comes first can help us work through conflict. Are we sliding into disunity? How can we settle the question without isolating members who disagree strongly? Just like members, groups can experience self-centeredness. When a group forgets its relationship to NA as a whole, it suffers—and the NA community suffers as well. One of the most destructive lies we tell ourselves is that our actions don't affect those around us. NA groups don't compete with each other; we work together for the greatest success for the greatest number.

It is remarkable how often in our groups—and in our lives—the lone voice is the one we most need to hear. Honoring the courage it takes to speak against a majority and giving serious consideration to the concerns raised doesn't just make us more inclusive; it also helps to ensure that the decisions we make are based in principle. Small changes that bring us to consensus are often the difference between a hasty decision and one that can last.

It may be helpful to remember what made us feel welcome, and what made us feel uneasy or alienated, when we first came to meetings. A meeting format is a vehicle for creating an atmosphere of recovery and establishing unity. The format can describe the meeting, tell a newcomer what is happening, and help the meeting run smoothly. Statements read in the format can make boundaries clear without being personal or accusatory. If formats are too cluttered with rules and instructions, they can overwhelm a meeting. On the other hand, careless or inattentive chairing can make a group feel unstable or unreliable. Mentorship can be as simple as ensuring that outgoing trusted servants stay on a few weeks after a new person is elected, and that time and attention can make all the difference in maintaining continuity and the atmosphere of recovery in a group.

Practicing unity and anonymity can be a struggle when the atmosphere of recovery is challenged. Personal conflicts between members, violence, and predatory behavior are very real issues in some groups. The service pamphlet *Disruptive and Violent Behavior* can be a useful resource—and so can other members. Confronting each other is part of how we help one another to recover, but it's a challenge to do that in a spirit of love and compassion. We address each other honestly and peacefully, and give each other room to grow. A member shared, "Unconditional love is not the same as unconditional acceptance. I don't have to like your behavior, but that doesn't mean we reject each other as human beings." Our common welfare means that every one of us needs every one of us. Every addict deserves the opportunity to recover. Our practice of unity helps us ensure that recovery is available to us all.

GROUP INVENTORY QUESTIONS _____

The questions below offer a way to begin—or continue—a service discussion or workshop focused on this Tradition.

1. What is our common welfare as a group? How does unity enhance our primary purpose?

2. What does the newcomer see and hear when attending our meeting? Is this an inviting group to join, or are we exclusive or intimidating in some way?

3. Do we make an effort to make everyone feel welcome? How do we welcome newcomers? Who are we missing and how can we include them?

4. How does sharing affect our group unity? Do we carry a clear message? How well do we listen to each other?

5. Does our group have a conscience, values, a personality? How can we embrace our differences and still practice unity? What do we do when we disagree?

6. Are we aware of any challenges to our group's unity? How can we better foster unity?

7. What's going on around us that affects our meeting? How can our group maintain an atmosphere of recovery when it's challenged? How do we address common challenges such as:

    • Newcomers from a facility arriving by the busload?

    • Helping addicts with young children hear a message when attending our meetings?

    • Members who are disruptive or deliberately disunifying?

    • Members who are threatening, intimidating, or predatory?

    • Members who feel threatened or afraid?

    • Breakups or conflict among our members?

    • Members who discriminate, or who exploit our differences for their own ends?

8. In what ways does this group contribute to NA unity locally and beyond? Is there anything we're doing that may be disunifying?

9. Are we in communication with our local service bodies? How can we help to improve the flow of information? Do our members participate in service, and communicate to the group about what's going on?

10. How does this Tradition help us understand anonymity? How does anonymity help us understand this Tradition? How do we practice anonymity in terms of this Tradition?

11. Discuss any bridges between this Tradition and other Traditions. What do these bridges teach us about our group?

12. What more can we do to bring the principles of this Tradition into our group efforts? What could we do differently to better fulfill our primary purpose?

In Service

When we come together in service, we connect with each other in a vital way. Most of us feel better when we are productive, and doing something together that helps addicts stay clean gives us a sense of belonging. The friendships we develop in service are unlike any in our lives—not because they are always easy or pleasant, but because we work hard, walk through struggles, and solve problems together. In contributing to our common welfare, we find meaning and joy. In creative action we find love and purpose.

Our vision statement includes the hope that every addict will be able to hear the message and that every member has the chance to "experience spiritual growth and fulfillment through service." We experience unity in service when we see our work as part of a greater whole, in service to our primary purpose, and connected to our personal recovery. In whatever way we serve, our vision must be at the center. We can be so focused on a task that we neglect to reach out to members who might be willing or interested. Vision is important, and we must constantly adjust our focus—zooming in on the task at hand, and pulling back to see how it fits in the larger frame.

Our experience, strength, and hope is our message. We share how NA works in our lives. When we're just going through the motions, we can feel it—and so can the newcomer. A hospitals and institutions (H&I) panel leader said, "I saw it intensely in H&I—someone would share the real struggle of staying clean, and everyone would connect. Another addict would share a bunch of clichés, and the whole room was watching the clock." Our common welfare depends on our willingness to be honest about our experience, and to share like our lives depend on it.

That honesty extends to the rest of our communication as well. Communication problems often arise because we're offering incomplete information, or we assume people aren't interested. Honesty is a commitment to reality. It can be hard to stay committed when reality is messy, complicated, or unpopular. Unity does not require uniformity, and it's often in allowing others to do things in their own way that new answers and questions come to light. Conflict can be a creative force as well as a challenge; active engagement sometimes helps to sharpen our thinking and spark excitement.

If service were easy, we wouldn't need so much literature on how to do it. Often we turn to the Traditions when we want to be right about something—or, more to the point, when we want to prove someone else wrong. "I would give what I thought were expert opinions about every Tradition, but over time I realized I was missing the point of the First," said one member. Learning to use our Traditions as a navigating system rather than a weapon is a shift for many of us. Making that shift has tremendous impact on our common welfare.

Many struggles in service reflect challenges we deal with in our personal lives. There is freedom in knowing we don't have to be in charge all the time. Not one of us is personally capable of guiding the affairs of NA. To keep our common welfare first, we let go of the desire to "own" a service position or a particular task, and we look to the good of the whole. Selfless service is our ideal, but we often struggle with our beliefs about our importance, our rightness, or our need for approval. One trusted servant remarked, "Every service meeting feels like one long Seventh Step workshop for me."

Being right can be its own addiction. Although we depend on each other's experience and insight, a constant stream of suggestions or second-guessing may be a sign of self-obsession. A member shared, "I was chairing a convention, and I thought my professional experience would be useful. I asked all the subcommittee chairs for budgets; I took them home and corrected them all. At the next meeting I returned the corrected copies to the subcommittee chairs. They were horrified, and I felt humiliated for overstepping my duties. The committee was willing to work through it with me, and eventually I was able to make amends and regain their trust."

We let each other do the work in our own way, and learn through it—with loving support, clear guidelines, and trust. Trust doesn't mean we stop paying attention. We can help each other stay on course and still believe we all share the same good intentions, even if we have different ways of getting there. We often judge others by their actions while judging ourselves by motives and intentions. Guidelines can keep us accountable without making it personal.

Thinking about principles before acting is never a mistake, but we can think ourselves right into a corner. We can get lost in policy and procedure and not get very much done at all. Enthusiasm can also be dangerous: In the rush to reach our goals, we sometimes resist group conscience or act impulsively. Experienced members have pointed out that nearly every early story about our Traditions began, "We had a great idea, and we meant well, but then . . . ." When we work together on a committee or workgroup, we are accountable to others, to the groups, and to our Higher Power; and often others are accountable to us. At times this can seem cumbersome or inefficient, but working together keeps us on track.

NA service is never a solo effort. Even when we are physically alone we are not spiritually isolated. We are connected to something larger, and our fellow addicts are often willing to help us if we are willing to ask. This is a "we" program, and we see it in action when we work together toward a goal. When we take the long view, we can trust that we're on a journey to a lesson. The outcome will speak for itself, if we let it. A member shared, "Every year I made the same motion to eliminate the area's convention, and every year a thousand addicts showed up. Who was I to keep fighting it? Finally it was time to let go."

Many of us have shared about the experience of carrying a conscience we did not agree with. It's a selfless act, and a spiritual exercise. When we can get out of the way and speak for our group or service body, we begin to experience what it can be like to let a Higher Power work through us. We start to have faith that the right thing will happen, even when we're not sure what that is, and come to understand that what is best for everyone will be best for us as well. We learn to communicate in a way that is honest and authentic without being aggressive. We can be ourselves without feeling like our selves are on the line.

WORKSHOP QUESTIONS _____

The questions below offer a way to begin—or continue—a service discussion or workshop focused on this Tradition.

1. How do the services we carry out benefit our common welfare? In what ways do we contribute to a sense of unity, locally and beyond?

2. What responsibilities does our service body have? Who do we serve? Who are we accountable to? How do accountability and responsibility help us to foster unity?

3. Does our NA community work together in a spirit of unity? How can we build or enhance a spirit of unity?

4. How do we recognize unity or disunity in our service body? How does disunity in NA affect us as a service body? What do we do about it? Do we do anything to acknowledge when we're doing well?

5. How does this Tradition help us understand anonymity? How does anonymity help us understand this Tradition? How do we practice anonymity in terms of this Tradition?

6. Discuss any bridges between this Tradition and one or more of the Twelve Concepts. What do these bridges teach us about our service efforts?

7. What more can we do to bring the principles of this Tradition into our service efforts? What could we do differently to better carry out our services?

The First Tradition makes clear that if we are to thrive as individual members, as groups, and as service committees, our common welfare—the good of NA as a whole—must be at the forefront of our consideration. Just as the description of our symbol in the Basic Text points out, "there is room within our universal program for all manifestations of the recovering person," there is room in Narcotics Anonymous for many different ways to live our principles, carry the message, and help NA grow and reach more addicts in more places. One size does not fit all, and unity does not equal uniformity. We don't have to do it like everyone else. Creative action of the spirit takes many shapes and forms throughout our Fellowship. Our personal recovery depends on NA unity. Our experience of unity in Narcotics Anonymous allows us to recover in an atmosphere of acceptance, freedom, and love. The freedom we gain as members of NA offers us courage to participate in the life and growth of our Fellowship.

For our group purpose there is but one ultimate authority—a loving God as He may express Himself in our group conscience. Our leaders are but trusted servants; they do not govern.

TRADITION

2

Whatever our views of a Higher Power, we can see a loving force at work in NA groups. Seeing the power available to us when we work together allows us to see it in our own lives as well. As we work the Steps, we learn to trust ourselves. When we are trustworthy, we begin to feel worthy. Recovery is as simple and as complicated as not lying to ourselves anymore. We can hear our own conscience.

Each of us is healthier in some ways than in others. We trust—and we use good sense. Living in fellowship with other addicts, we learn discernment. The person we feel safe to talk to when our heart hurts may not be the same person we would choose to be our group treasurer. Trusting is an act of love. Giving that gift is a choice each of us makes for ourselves.

The Second Tradition assures us that NA will be there for us no matter what. When we have a reservation in our Second Tradition, we don't quite believe that all will be well. We fear that we have the ability to destroy Narcotics Anonymous. If something particular happens—if we take this action or pass that motion or even listen to a scary idea— NA will die. Our experience shows us that NA is strong enough to withstand our growing pains. Tradition Two tells us that we can trust a Power greater than ourselves. We learn to stand up for a principle without feeling like we're fighting for our lives.

When we trust the process, we are free to participate in it. We are safe to act in unity, speak our conscience from a place of love, and hear the voice of a Higher Power.

Tradition Two

The Second Tradition is clear and freeing. It begins with the group, united by common purpose. But it immediately makes clear that neither the group nor its members are in charge. Tradition Two sets an ultimate authority above us all, freeing us from the need either to be an authority or to submit to someone else's control. Under the loving care of a Power greater than ourselves we are all equal, and we are each important to NA as a whole.

In many ways, the Second Tradition can be said to embody the spirit of all twelve. Unity, purpose, selfless service, relationship to a God of our understanding, conscience, and anonymity are principles that shape the Second Tradition and our way of life. The better we understand this Tradition, the more clearly we understand what NA has to offer—and what it asks of us.

Service is any action through which we give of ourselves, and every service position is a stewardship of trust. We do not govern; we also do not own service positions, boards, committees—or meetings. When we come together in unity, we shine. A connected group conscience recognizes the value of all its members. One member described leadership in NA as "holding a space for the brilliance of others." Allowing that brilliance to come through can be challenging: It requires us to listen, to reserve judgment, and to be open to new answers even when we are really committed to old ones.

Many of us struggle to reconcile the idea of leadership put forth by this Tradition with our concerns about authority and control. The most powerful way we lead in NA is by example. The Basic Text reminds us in Step Twelve that "the temptation to give advice is great, but when we do so we lose the respect of newcomers." Tradition Two tells us that leadership in NA will never be a position of authority; when we lead we are servants. Practicing responsibility and selflessness together opens the door to the spiritual gift of anonymity.

The Tradition speaks of "group conscience," and within NA there are varied understandings of what that means. Some members believe that the only place group conscience exists is in the NA groups. Others see it more broadly. Our group purpose—like our common welfare—is one of the ties that bind us together, a unifying thread that weaves through everything we do in NA. In this view, the process of coming to a decision as a service board or committee is no less spiritual than in groups. Each member, and each group, is entitled to their own understanding.

Honoring group conscience is a spiritual exercise. Sometimes listening to the group is easy and gratifying. When we sit in a business meeting and learn about practicing principles, we can be glad we're there. When a newer member teaches us something we hadn't quite understood before, we may be amazed at the power of the program. We serve by being present and meeting the needs of the group as expressed by its conscience. The love and unity we feel as a result are rewards for the time and energy we give in service to NA.

When we disagree with a decision or a direction, honoring that conscience is much more challenging. We will not always get our way, and letting go can be a struggle. The Second Tradition asks us to let go of our self-obsession and desire for control. Group conscience serves as a compass, guiding us through the challenges we face together. There are times when we must find the courage to be the lone voice on an issue or stand up for principle against a strong majority. We choose our battles wisely. If we notice that we are the lone voice on every issue, we may want to consider the utility of acceptance and surrender as spiritual principles. Listening to guidance and acting accordingly demonstrates both courage and humility. We listen to our own conscience, to each other, and to the needs of the group for the guidance of a Higher Power, expressed as group conscience.

One way to understand group conscience is as a collective awareness of spiritual principles. When each of us listens carefully to our own conscience and pays attention to each other, we develop a common voice and shared wisdom. When we listen for a Higher Power in our decision making, our decisions improve. When we foster awareness, it grows. The group becomes greater than the sum of its parts.

WORD BY WORD

Define, expand on, or clarify the words or phrases from this Tradition, one at a time or in relation to each other, for writing or discussion with your sponsor or other NA members.

Example: servant

To be a *servant* may mean attending to others in a relationship of inequality, but this is not the only way to understand the term, nor is it the meaning that applies when we use the term in NA. Other meanings of the word include a person who is devoted, is useful or beneficial, cares for others, or works toward a purpose. A *servant* acts with care and devotion. It is a role of trust, not authority. We use this language because no individual is ever to have sole ownership over any part of NA. We serve our Fellowship in humility and gratitude, recognizing the importance of everyone's contributions. When we strive to serve selflessly, our purpose, rather than our personality, is primary. The task, purpose, and process are all spiritual.

Serving changes us. Just as making amends teaches us to be more forgiving, selfless service brings generosity, compassion, and awareness of purpose. Service is practice for how we live in the world. It's an opportunity to give what has been so freely given to us, and to recognize how much effort goes into the blessings we take for granted in and out of Narcotics Anonymous.

SPIRITUAL PRINCIPLES

Each Tradition embodies a variety of spiritual principles. The list of principles and values below may be useful as we consider applications of this Tradition. Explore them in writing or discussion with your sponsor or other NA members. If other principles or values not listed below seem relevant for you, include those as well.

• unity	• surrender	• acceptance	• commitment
• selflessness	• love	• anonymity	• safety
• hospitality	• empathy	• goodwill	• humility

Example: love

Love is one of the driving forces in Narcotics Anonymous, and yet Tradition Two is the only Tradition in which the word *love* appears. The loving spirit that binds us together is greater than our individual personalities. A spirit of love gives life to anonymity, allowing us to come together in unity. Being a trusted servant, acting in a spirit of love, and trusting a Power greater than ourselves are all part of practicing this Tradition. The love we share in NA means we care enough to save each other's lives. The most loving things we do for each other aren't always easy or gentle. We try to approach each other and our service with kindness, care, and concern, and to find courage to reach out to each other with honesty and compassion.

Regardless of who we are, where we've been, or what we've done, we find in Narcotics Anonymous a place of empathy, acceptance, welcome, and belonging. We don't find it with everyone, but anonymity frees us to experience love, and that love, in turn, frees us to accept one another without reservation. The Second Tradition tells us that a loving God may express Himself in our group conscience, but it's hard to hear a loving God when we are being unloving. Unity depends on our willingness to keep coming from love, even when that seems like the hardest thing to do. It's a spiritual exercise that changes us, and a spiritual commitment that ensures our survival.

For Members

Each of us has a conscience, that quiet voice that guides us. At its root, the word *conscience* means "to know within oneself." Developing our personal conscience is a process that continues as long as we are clean. Many of us begin recovery with a distorted sense of right and wrong. Our moral compass had been so skewed by our addiction that we had trouble following its guidance. Reconnecting with our conscience often begins by taking on the values of others. Learning to see from another's point of view helps build empathy, but it also teaches us to see new possibilities. Things can look very different from another angle of vision. While our sponsor, our family, and our community all provide us with models, ultimately we must learn to know within ourselves. Through the Steps we develop our own values and tools for recognizing when we are on course and when we are drifting. Often this begins as a set of absolutes: right or wrong, up or down, and that's the end of it. Gradually, we start to see shades of color where there had once been only black and white, and as we mature we are more able to tolerate mixed feelings. There can be many different right answers to the same question. Changing our angle of vision changes what we see. Our perspective shapes our perception, and our perception helps determine our experience.

When we come together to make decisions for NA, we listen together for guidance from a Higher Power. Learning to listen takes practice and patience. We hear our conscience in the ideas of fellow members. Our personal recovery contributes to the conscience of the group. In meditation, meetings, and service, we learn that silence can allow us to hear the quiet voice of truth within.

Our practice of the Second Tradition begins among other recovering addicts who share our principles. As we serve together, a bond develops. The friendships forged in service can be some of the deepest in our lives. The time spent and trust developed in service give us the opportunity to share deeply with one another. Intimacy develops through shared experience. Despite differences of opinion or style, we are united by our love for Narcotics Anonymous and our shared sense of responsibility for our primary purpose.

Being a trusted servant goes against everything addiction demands of us. This is one reason why being of service is such a powerful part of recovery. In much the same way that making amends teaches us to be more forgiving, the practice of being a trusted servant brings us generosity, compassion, and awareness of our purpose.

We may not experience the same unity of purpose with people in other areas of our lives. Outside of NA, people are not bound by our Traditions, but they have principles and values of their own. We can apply the principles of this Tradition as we relate to those around us. When we look for common ground, common guidance, and common purpose with others, our relationship with the world can shift dramatically.

The Second Tradition offers freedom from self-centeredness by helping us practice being a part of, rather than apart from. A simple change in perspective can offer profound improvements in our relationships. Our lives can become more harmonious and loving when we consider our group purpose at home or at work; when we are willing to allow an ultimate authority above the situation and to listen for that voice; when we approach our work, families, or community organizations with a willingness to serve and cooperate rather than govern.

The same tools we use to be happy, productive members of a group can help us to experience unity and a sense of belonging in other areas of our lives. One member shared about learning to practice Tradition Two at home. "My sponsor suggested I try approaching my relationship like a coffee commitment: to show up and do my part in a spirit of selfless service. I thought I was being asked to be submissive, but the opposite was true: I got free from the idea that relationships were about winning and losing." When we ask how to be of service rather than how we can be served, it's much easier to find serenity. "It wasn't easy and I wasn't consistent," the member added. "But that shift meant that my actions weren't just about me or my partner anymore, but about my relationship with my Higher Power as I could express it at home. It became a way for me to learn about love, trust, service, and developing a group conscience that would serve everyone in the household." Practicing these principles in all our affairs can bring freedom in all areas of our lives.

Tradition Two offers a spirituality any of us can put into practice. Together, group conscience and conscious contact bring our relationship with a Higher Power into our decisions, actions, and relationships at every level. Finding that bridge between Tradition Two and Step Eleven changes us at our core. We learn to trust, to be trustworthy, to give freely, and to lead humbly. NA service is how we give back what was so freely given to us. Together we seek our Higher Power's will and the power to carry that out. We know what it feels like to be in harmony with that conscience. All of that is good practice for how to live in the world.

QUESTIONS FOR MEMBERS _____

The questions below offer a way to begin—or continue—the process of writing, reflection, and discussion of this Tradition with your sponsor or other NA members.

IN NA

1. What is a conscience, and how do I get in touch with mine? What does group conscience mean to me, and how do I participate in it? What is the difference between the group conscience and my individual conscience?

2. How does participating in group conscience help develop my sense of a Higher Power? How do I allow my Higher Power to influence my decision making? What helps me cultivate that influence?

3. How does my understanding of open-mindedness help me apply the Second Tradition? How do I encourage or welcome the ideas of new members? Do I consider the needs or views of those who aren't in the room? How do I find the courage to ask difficult questions in business meetings?

4. How do I set aside my personal preferences in favor of an emerging consensus? What is the difference between surrender and abdication of responsibility?

5. Is my behavior in group business meetings consistent with the principles of this Tradition? Do I use my cleantime or position to intimidate others or to assert authority? Do I listen or do I just want to talk? How do I find the balance?

6. What part does my Higher Power play in my service efforts and as a member of a home group? How does faith allow me to carry out the group's conscience even if I disagree with it?

7. What are the attributes of a trusted servant? Which of these do I act on or strive for?

8. What is the difference between governing and leadership? As a trusted servant, how am I a leader? How do I practice leadership in my home group? How can I practice leadership in a spirit of anonymity? When am I most likely to try to govern?

9. How does this Tradition help me understand anonymity? How does anonymity help me understand this Tradition? How do I practice anonymity in terms of this Tradition?

10. Describe any bridges between this Tradition and one or more of the Twelve Steps. What do these bridges teach me about my recovery?

11. What more can I do to put the principles of this Tradition into action? How would applying this Tradition change my attitudes and actions?

IN ALL OUR AFFAIRS

12. How have I applied this Tradition outside NA? How else might the principles of this Tradition guide my thinking or my actions?

13. Are there other areas in my life where I can see the value of a conscience, or where I can see a conscience emerging? How do I listen for what I know as group conscience in my relationships outside of NA?

14. Does my history with authority influence my experience today? How does my belief in an ultimate authority change my perspective?

15. How do I practice this Tradition when others are not bound by it?

16. Am I open to hearing truth from any source, or am I distracted by prejudices? How does practicing the principles of this Tradition open me to hearing others?

17. How important is it to me to be liked? Do I ever compromise my sense of what is right in order to please others?

18. Am I worthy of trust? How can I practice trustworthiness today?

19. How can I remain humble and open-minded even when I'm sure I'm right?

20. When a decision doesn't go my way, how do I come to believe that all will be well? How does my attitude reflect my acceptance?

21. In what other areas of my life might this Tradition be useful? What other opportunities are there for me to seek group conscience?

For Groups

The NA group is at the heart of this Tradition, and this Tradition explains the practical spirituality at the heart of NA groups. Our groups have purpose and conscience. They are the primary vehicle for our message. Everything we do to help an addict get the message is service. Service begins when we put ourselves aside and welcome the newcomer. That simple action might be the most important thing we ever do. Our leaders are servants we trust; like the group, they operate under the authority of a loving God. When a group is clear on its purpose, its ultimate authority, and its message, the rest has a way of falling into place.

We invite a Higher Power to influence our decisions. When we listen for the voice of a Higher Power in each other, we hear one another with an open mind. Some of us bring experience; some bring fresh perspectives. Each is necessary. The Second Tradition invites us to practice anonymity by separating ideas from the people who express them. We can disagree with each other's ideas without putting each other down. For many of us this is the first time that we can disagree strongly without feeling that we must leave, or that we are no longer welcome. Each of us is part of group conscience, regardless of our personality or our opinion.

Just as individual conscience is a matter of knowing within ourselves, group conscience is coming to know within the group. Group conscience expresses itself as unity and goodwill, and is reflected in the simple decisions that define a group: How are the chairs arranged? Are there refreshments? Is there a greeter at the door? Many of these decisions occur in the group's business meeting, and each reflects the conscience of the group. Group conscience is not the same as group opinion, and not the same as a vote. Each of these can be an expression of the group's conscience, but conscience is never limited to the business meeting. Over time, handling ordinary business and addressing challenges, a group develops an identity and values of its own. In group conscience, we experience unity in action. We begin to understand how unconditional love might actually work.

Time is an essential ingredient for cultivating group conscience. Having patience for discussion, or waiting until the next meeting before moving forward with a decision, saves the energy and goodwill lost when hasty actions have consequences. Some ideas need to simmer. We practice humility and open-mindedness by letting our Higher Power influence our thinking over time. We consult experienced members, remembering that despite different levels of experience we are all equal in Narcotics Anonymous.

We see the outcome of group conscience in the atmosphere we create before the meeting begins, during and after the meeting, and in our business meetings. We can't measure group conscience, but we can feel it. A strong group tends to be consistent and recognizable not just in its format but in its values. We can sense the difference between a meeting that's spiritually based and one that's personality-driven. The spoken message may be the same, but the atmosphere of recovery is different.

We create boards and committees so groups aren't weighed down with decisions that will divert us from our primary purpose. However, groups have a responsibility: The Second Concept reminds us that "the final authority and responsibility for service rests with the NA groups." Groups find a balance between meeting that responsibility and delegating appropriately. Some groups are more actively involved than others, but issues sometimes arise that demand the attention of many more groups than usual. When a group has been disconnected from local services for a while, decisions may seem surprising or even alarming. Just as it is important for service bodies to find the time and the words to inform the groups, it is important for the groups to stay in touch with NA services.

We ask our servants at every level to invite a loving Power into decision making and then to act in accordance with those decisions. When we ask a member to serve, we have a responsibility to them and to the group to support them as best we can, offering help and guidance. The better we define the task or project, the easier it is to do it well. Clear guidelines and formats are most effective when they support trusted servants rather than restrict them.

We count on our group trusted servants to ensure that the meeting format is followed, and to pay attention to how the meeting is running. Chairing a meeting is a form of leadership. Leaders emerge naturally in any group. But in NA, leadership never means that a single member or group is in command. A controlling attitude can easily drive away the newcomer. Learning to participate without trying to control can be very difficult for some of us.

A member suggested that "when I try to be the ultimate authority of my group, I do more harm than good, even when I have something valuable to offer." Protecting the group from the power of our own personalities doesn't mean that we hide ourselves away; we lead by example rather than by instruction or imposition. Newer members gain experience when more experienced members encourage, respect, and value their input. Rather than having to compete to victory or defeat every time a decision is on the table, we create an open, accepting atmosphere in which solutions naturally arise.

We feel included when we are asked to be of service by setting up chairs, greeting people, sweeping the floors, or arranging the literature on the table. That experience can change the course of lives. When the newcomer feels trusted and has a part to play in the life of the group, both the group and the addict have a better chance at survival.

When we help to start a meeting or an NA community, we may be in a strong position of leadership. If we are wise, we help those around us learn to take on responsibility. We are on the lookout for opportunities to share that leadership among others in the growing community. If we hold on too long or too tightly, we may find our position removed from us—either because the community outgrows the need, or because we sicken under the weight. Our understanding of anonymity may be clouded by a sense of importance. We start to feel resentful. We might not recognize how unattractive this lack of humility can be until we find ourselves outside, looking in. We need to remember to work together and to ask for help. Listening carefully for the voice of a loving Higher Power expressed in our group conscience leads to healthy groups, and healthy groups are powerful. We are a force for good in the lives of addicts, in our communities, and in the world.

GROUP INVENTORY QUESTIONS _____

The questions below offer ways to begin—or continue—group inventory or discussion focused on this Tradition.

1. What is our group purpose? How do our decisions help us further our purpose?

2. How do we invite a loving Higher Power into our decision-making process?

3. What is our shared understanding of group conscience? Is it the same as or different from a majority vote or consensus? How does our group establish a group conscience?

4. What is the relationship between anonymity and the group conscience? Why is it important that everyone be heard? How do we invite full participation? How do newcomers contribute to group conscience?

5. How does our group conscience moderate the influence of strong personalities or people perceived to be authorities? Do we ensure that all points of view are heard before we make a decision? How do we distinguish between leadership and governing?

6. How do we balance collective and individual conscience? How do we recognize when group conscience has been reached?

7. When and how might we revisit or rethink our decisions?

8. What does our group do to ensure that group conscience meetings maintain a spiritual focus and foster goodwill?

9. What role do spiritual principles play in the decision-making processes of our group? When a problem arises, how do we find a solution? How does our group ask itself difficult questions or handle unresolved issues? How do we recognize when we're moving too fast or too slow when making a decision?

10. What are some of the leadership qualities we seek among trusted servants in our group? How do these qualities demonstrate our spiritual principles? How do we cultivate those qualities in one another?

11. How can we balance rotation and continuity? How do home group members lead even when they're not holding specific service positions?

12. What is our responsibility to our trusted servants? How can the group support a trusted servant who feels isolated, overwhelmed, or unprepared? What's the right balance for our group between trust and accountability?

13. How does this Tradition help us understand anonymity? How does anonymity help us understand this Tradition? How do we practice anonymity in terms of this Tradition?

14. Discuss any bridges between this Tradition and other Traditions. What do these bridges teach us about our group?

15. What more can we do to bring the principles of this Tradition into our group efforts? What could we do differently to better fulfill our primary purpose?

In Service

Groups focus on our primary purpose: to carry the message to the addict who still suffers. Service beyond the group carries out some secondary purposes: creating meeting lists, getting literature into facilities, or putting on a dance. Each of these, in turn, supports our primary purpose. NA service is always connected in some way to our group purpose, and is under the same direction: Our leaders do not govern, service is not authority, and the ability to serve depends on the trust of those around us.

When we need to make a decision, it can be helpful to talk about spiritual principles. Spiritual principles can be a lens through which we examine ideas. Actions taken in anger, resentment, or haste tend to create trouble down the road. Taking time to consider principles may not change a decision, but it may change the way we carry it out—and that can make all the difference.

There are differing practices of group conscience within our Fellowship. Some members believe that the key word in the phrase is *group,* and that the conscience described in the Second Tradition exists only in the NA groups as described in *The Group Booklet.* Because this view holds that the conscience resides in the group, all decisions should go back to the home groups whenever possible. It requires careful planning, because the simplest decisions can take months to make and excellent communication between groups and service bodies. Although service boards and committees are always accountable to the groups as well as to a Higher Power, not all groups enjoy exercising that authority on a day-to-day basis. It can distract from the primary purpose of the groups, and is liable to slow service efforts. Many NA communities operate differently, and values and practices vary widely across the Fellowship.

In other places, a broader understanding of "group conscience" allows for the understanding that what happens in service bodies is no less spiritual than what happens in NA groups. One member asked how it could be that an authority so powerful could be expressed only in one possible outlet; for him, the idea that conscience was restricted to one level of service put unnecessary limitations on the understanding of a Higher Power.

Many of us have been parts of service bodies or committees that seemed to operate out of a shared understanding of purpose and values that was consistent across the committee and across time—much like a strong home group. The experience of being part of a committee or workgroup that takes on this kind of momentum can be exciting, but it's important to remember our lines of accountability in NA service. Participants may feel the conscience of a service body in its consensus and enthusiasm, but maintaining communication and inclusion in our communities is essential.

When consensus inside a committee doesn't match consensus outside that committee, disunity can result. Often the result is not open conflict but a simple fading of energy. If service is not attractive or inclusive, our efforts tend to last a while and then fizzle out. When energy and enthusiasm are fading, we can often look to the Second Tradition to understand why.

The times when we are most passionate about a particular issue in service may also be when we're most at risk of becoming closed-minded or being led astray—and least likely to see those risks for ourselves. Passion for service is a gift, and there are certainly times we do need to stand up for principle. During these moments, staying in touch with the spirit of goodwill that guides our service is a must. We need to keep an eye on our passion, lest it become self-righteousness; and we keep an eye on our disagreements, lest we begin to harbor ill will toward our fellows. Vigilance is an inside job. We ask ourselves about our sense of proportion: Does the size of our feelings match the size of the issue?

The Second Tradition doesn't exempt us from the need sometimes to protect our program "from the internal and external forces that may destroy us," but it reminds us that we are not the ultimate authority in NA. It can be surprising when an emotional conflict leads to a renewal of faith, but when a storm passes, the resilience of our Fellowship and the love we feel within it can bring us to a new level of surrender. We can trust NA to survive, even when growing pains are severe.

We are much more productive when we build structures in which responsibilities are outlined, roles are clear, and simple checks are in place as a part of the process. Mentoring, supporting, and encouraging members in their efforts to serve can simply make it easier to do the next right thing. Accountability is a two-way street. When our relationship to our services lacks trust, service is unattractive.

Leadership—in a group, on a committee, or simply in performing a specific task—is an honor, a privilege, and a form of service. We must understand and honor the limits on our role and the difference between service and government. If we confuse them, we are generally not confused for long: NA communities have a tendency to correct that behavior, sometimes in pretty ungentle ways. For ourselves as well as our Fellowship, it's important that we recognize the difference between getting things done and governing. When we honor the trust placed in us, leadership and service can be one and the same.

WORKSHOP QUESTIONS

The questions below offer a way to begin—or continue—a service discussion or workshop focused on this Tradition.

1. Does a service body have a group conscience? How do we exercise group conscience in service? How do we invite a loving Higher Power into our decisions?

2. What does a good group conscience process look like? What would an observer notice about decision making in our service body?

3. How best do we involve groups in our process? How does our work impact other service bodies? What's the relationship between communication and Tradition Two?

4. How does our service body practice spiritual principles in our work and in our meetings? How do we allow a loving Higher Power to guide our process and service efforts?

5. What are the risks of uniformity in our decision-making process? How do we consider different perspectives as we make decisions? Do we ensure that minority voices are honored? Do we consider the views of those who cannot or do not speak for themselves?

6. How does our understanding of anonymity help us apply the Second Tradition? Are there people or ideas we are unwilling to hear? How do we reconcile the need to hear many viewpoints with our desire for efficiency and simplicity?

7. What is the difference between practicing patience and avoiding a discussion or decision? Do we rush into decisions or discuss them until we arrive at a solution? What is the value of listening to all viewpoints? How does our service benefit or suffer from the quality of our discussions?

8. Is involvement in our service body increasing or decreasing? How might this be connected to the decisions we've been making or the ways we've been making them?

9. How do we see a Higher Power working through us in service? Do we trust that all will be well? What are our reservations about that?

10. What are some differences between being a servant and being a trusted servant? How does that change our attitudes and actions?

11. What does leadership mean in Narcotics Anonymous? How is that different from its usual meanings?

12. What is the difference between leading and governing? What can we do to ensure that trusted servants lead rather than control? What can we do if a member is trying to govern or dominate a group or a service body? How can we balance rotation and continuity?

13. How does this Tradition help us understand anonymity? How does anonymity help us understand this Tradition? How do we practice anonymity in terms of this Tradition?

14. Discuss any bridges between this Tradition and one or more of the Twelve Concepts. What do these bridges teach us about our service efforts?

15. What more can we do to bring the principles of this Tradition into our service efforts? What could we do differently to better carry out our services?

It's extraordinary for an addict to get clean. In NA, we not only get clean but recover together in unity, carry a message, and fulfill service obligations. Tradition Two tells us this is possible because we are united under an ultimate authority. This Tradition frees each of us from the dangerous belief that we are in charge, or that some of us are more important than others. Seeing this Tradition at work in our groups offers a vision of hope. As we apply Tradition Two in our service—and in our lives—we begin to understand the power and grace available to us in surrender.

*The only requirement for membership
is a desire to stop using.*

TRADITION

3

There is only one requirement for membership, but membership will require much of us. Tradition Three swings the door to Narcotics Anonymous wide open and invites an opening in our own hearts. As long as we have a desire to stop using drugs, our right to membership in NA is unconditional. We may attend meetings for a long time before deciding to be members. When we make that decision, our lives begin to change.

Working the Steps deepens our understanding of membership. We begin with surrender; we find hope; we make a decision. The Third Tradition confronts us with our prejudices, control issues, insecurities, and fears. It also reveals generosity, compassion, and empathy. Openness calls for a change of heart. Our minds may change quickly, but to change our hearts we have to humbly ask. The more real we get, the more willing we are to let go of our defects, secrets, and resentments. We make amends and clean up after ourselves so we don't have to drag our shame and fear around anymore. Because our membership in NA is secure, we are free to be honest about who we are.

NA membership creates connection and belonging. We are a part of something greater than ourselves, and it changes us. There is no single way to be an NA member, no model of the recovering addict.

The most powerful message we carry is the simple truth of our experience. Our real value is in being ourselves. We are the message of hope.

Tradition Three

At the heart of Tradition Three is compassion. This Tradition ensures that every addict is free to decide whether to be a member. Through some combination of desperation, courage, anguish, and hope, we find willingness. Desire is not always visible and it is not measurable. Whether our commitment to NA is shallow or profound, above all it is ours. No one can tell us it is or is not good enough, or that we are or are not "NA material." The door is always open; we can make or unmake that decision at any time. When we surrender, our lives begin to change. After that first surrender there will be many more—and after that first decision to be a member, we will commit and recommit, over and over. Life circumstances—a move, a breakup, change or controversy within the Fellowship—can lead us to question our membership. It can take as much courage to recommit to NA as it does to make that decision the first time.

Our fundamental equality, expressed through the principle of anonymity, doesn't mean that differences disappear or don't matter. We can recover in unity. Our differences deepen our ability to be of service. Our principles allow NA to transcend difficult and sometimes painful issues of diversity. We are often surprised at where we find common ground.

We tell newcomers we are only interested in "what you want to do about your problem and how we can help." Practicing Tradition Three puts that into action. Our symbol reminds us that the broader the base, the higher the point of freedom. Our diverse membership, around the world and within our home communities, can help to ensure that there is someone to welcome every addict who comes in. Empathy and dignity are available to all.

Recovery is not automatic. Our literature states, "If you want what we have to offer *and are willing to make the effort to get it*, then you are ready to take certain steps." Lives depend on the answer to these critical questions: Do I want what NA has to offer? Am I willing to make the effort? We may be tempted to think we can answer these questions for others, but no one knows the depth of an addict's desire. An addict who comes around for months or years without putting cleantime together might be desperate to get it; an addict who gets clean right away and whose life comes right back together might not take the process seriously. We have no way of knowing for someone else.

When others question their membership, especially when a family member or beloved sponsee is making that decision, we want them to choose freely—

but we want them to choose our way. It can help us to consider that we are simply practicing patience, waiting (and hoping and praying) that their time will come. Tradition Three teaches us patience. We welcome people back with love and respect, sometimes for years. We can be loving and still tell each other what we see. We are each other's eyes and ears. When our observations are offered with respect and care, they are more likely to be heard.

We approach this Tradition from both sides of the door: as addicts considering whether NA is a place we want to be, and as members deciding how best to carry the message. Our message is clear. Questioning or trying to place limits on the openness of this Tradition has been a part of our history from the very beginning. Much of our attention to the Third Tradition reflects our reservations about its simplicity. Protecting ourselves and our program doesn't mean guarding the door, but making sure it stays open, setting aside ideas of who should be here and why. Not all who come will want what NA has, and not all will be willing to do the work. It is never our job to judge another addict's desire for recovery. Membership issues have a way of resolving themselves. We pay attention to our own motives and behavior and remember that actions mean more than words.

WORD BY WORD

Define, expand on, or clarify the words or phrases from this Tradition, one at a time or in relation to each other, for writing or discussion with your sponsor or other NA members.

Example: only

Only is a short word that packs a lot of power. It derives from the word *one*, and it means solely or exclusively or without exception. In other Traditions, less absolute words are used: *ought* and *should* appear over and over. We talk about our *primary* purpose, not our sole or exclusive purpose. In contrast, the Third Tradition is clear: The *only* requirement for membership is a desire to stop using.

SPIRITUAL PRINCIPLES

Each Tradition embodies a variety of spiritual principles. The list of principles and values below may be useful as we consider applications of this Tradition. Explore them in writing or discussion with your sponsor or other NA members. If other principles or values not listed below seem relevant for you, include those as well.

- tolerance
- patience
- willingness
- courage
- service

- compassion
- generosity
- inclusiveness
- responsibility
- love

- anonymity
- welcome
- faith
- open-mindedness

- humility
- equality
- trust
- acceptance

Example: welcome

The white chips and keytags we give to newcomers include the word *welcome*. The practice of hospitality, or welcome, is important to many faiths and cultures. The act of welcoming others changes us. We begin by welcoming people to meetings. Simply making eye contact or offering a hug to a newcomer can make all the difference to them—and to us. Many of us have memories of peering through the blinds, fearful of the mail carrier or the neighbors or shadows. Many of us know what it's like to sit frozen as the phone rings or the door knocks or the dog barks, waiting for whoever it is to please go away. Feeling welcome, and welcoming others to our new way of life, helps us see the world as a less hostile place. Practicing welcome as a spiritual principle can change our relationship to NA, and to the world outside.

For Members

Tradition Three asks us to practice open-mindedness toward ourselves, toward others, and toward the possibility of change. NA was "the last house on the block" for many of us; we had nowhere left to go. It's not an empty house, though. We need to make room, and make peace, with people we would probably never encounter anywhere else. We may be scared of each other; we may have history; we may have prejudices or blind spots that we are perfectly comfortable with. Chapter Eight in the Basic Text reminds us, however, that "addiction makes us one of a kind." The Third Tradition asks us to examine our motives and beliefs, our trust and ability to love, our open-mindedness, willingness, faith, and courage in carrying the message.

Each of us experiences membership in our own way, but it begins with the awareness that it's time to stop using. This is the same admission that fuels our First Step. The price of admission is an admission: To be a member, we admit that we have a problem and want to do something about it. When we surrender in our hearts, recovery begins. Our relationships with other addicts change; our experience of meetings changes; our perception changes. The admission in Step One and the decision in Tradition Three are part of the same surrender.

While Narcotics Anonymous is a program for drug addicts seeking recovery, our First Step focuses not on the drugs we used, but on the disease of addiction. For some members, Tradition Three offers a way to think about the actions and attitudes that make us unhappy long after we stop using drugs. Getting in touch with the desire to stop using once we are clean may be about other ways we use—people, places, things, feelings, behaviors, drama—to avoid facing ourselves. For other members, this type of thinking feels like a distraction from our primary purpose. Whatever our perspective, the fact remains: Addiction may be arrested but not cured, and no matter how far we are from our last one, each of us is one bad decision away from the next one.

As our relationship to our own desire evolves, so does our thinking about membership. Membership begins with desire, but it doesn't end there. This Tradition allows us to ask questions from different perspectives: What does it mean to me to be a member? How do I allow someone else to be a member? The Third Tradition essay in *It Works: How and Why* cautions, we are "not the jury of desire." A member who had come around for years without ever accumulating much cleantime said, "I never did the program like people wanted me to, but I'd have died years ago if I hadn't come at all." Finding the patience and tolerance to accept those members we can't seem to stop judging is an exercise in surrender, acceptance, and humility.

Examining our beliefs about membership offers new perspectives on our commitments at home, at work, in our friendships, and in Narcotics Anonymous. We recognize responsibilities of membership in areas of our lives we had not previously considered. We may find reservations we didn't know we had, or limits we put in place—almost without noticing—in order to protect ourselves from harm. Those protections may no longer serve us.

We become and maintain a community by getting together in lots of different ways besides meetings. Little gestures can help us feel connected. Many of us remember the first time we were invited to coffee after a meeting. Feeling noticed and included is important to us. We are responsible to include new people in these activities. There are no requirements on our social lives, but when we are so immersed in our circle of friends that we don't notice new faces around us, we turn people away without even knowing they were there. One of the most significant ways we deny someone membership is to ignore them.

Each of us has a part to play in making NA groups welcoming to everyone. Doing so requires checking our reservations about the recovery of others. A newcomer may seem too young or too old, or too beaten down or not having lost enough; they may have done the wrong drug, or not used like we did; they may still be on parole, or take medication we have opinions about. They may be criminals; they may be clergy or law enforcement; they may look at us in a way that gives us the creeps. Addicts may be clean a long time and still not be socially skilled or socially acceptable; they may work their program in a way that seems different or even threatening to us. There is no model of the recovering addict, no profile of the addict who suffers, and no condition on membership besides desire—which is between the addict and their Higher Power. The miracle of recovery is available to us all, even after we've been clean a long time. Just as we see the miracle of addicts getting clean, we see the miracle of clean addicts getting better, sometimes after many years. Allowing each other to change after we have known each other a long time takes faith, compassion, and open-mindedness.

Each of us is better at reaching out at some times and in some ways than at others. It's good there are so many of us. People who come in and out are easier for some of us to accept than those steadily attending while on drug replacement therapy; others of us are exceptionally good at reaching out to the newcomer, but have no patience for those who seek help elsewhere as well as in NA. Sometimes a member hurts us, directly or indirectly, in the course of a relapse, or they may be locked in a behavior or pattern for which we simply cannot feel compassion. We reach out where we can, and make an effort to increase our compassion for those who don't match our expectations or whose recovery doesn't look like our own.

We find a home in NA, and then we find a home inside that home. Within the wide, weird, colorful world of NA membership, we find our tribe. If something changes—a breakup, a move, a death—and that group is no longer the center of our recovering life, we expand our horizons and our network. We find ways to give back, to make sure that our Fellowship is always growing—and we're always growing, too. Our Fellowship keeps us alive and free, and the work we do to help it grow ensures that there will continue to be members and meetings here when we need them.

QUESTIONS FOR MEMBERS

The questions below offer a way to begin—or continue—the process of writing, reflection, and discussion of this Tradition with your sponsor or other NA members.

IN NA

1. What brought me to make the decision to be a member of NA?
   What does "a desire to stop using" mean for me in my recovery today?
   Do I want what NA has to offer?

2. What was it like for me when I came to my first meetings? What are some of the things that I experienced that helped me choose to become a member? What can I do to help the newcomer make that choice for themselves?

3. What does membership in NA mean to me? What happens when I make the decision to become a member? What are my responsibilities as a member? Have they changed over time? Do I try to hold others to the standards I set for myself?

4. How do my actions and attitudes reflect my decision to be a member of NA? How is it evident when I share, in my willingness to help the newcomer, in my behavior in and around meetings, or in how I serve in NA?

5. What part can I play in creating an inviting atmosphere? How does it feel to be a part of a group that addicts want to come back to?

6. Have I ever given someone a reason not to come back to a Narcotics Anonymous meeting? How do I remain welcoming when I'm just not feeling it?

7. When have I judged other addicts? What happens when I try to determine who will stay clean and who won't? What are the consequences for me, for other members, and for the addict who still suffers?

8. What expectations do I have about how others recover and serve in NA? Are these expectations related to NA principles or my own opinions?

9. What are some of my reservations about our open membership policy? What additional qualifications do my actions and behavior impose on people's membership and recovery? How do I reach out with compassion and lack of judgment?

10. How does this Tradition help me understand anonymity? How does anonymity help me understand this Tradition? How do I practice anonymity in terms of this Tradition?

11. Describe any bridges between this Tradition and one or more of the Twelve Steps. What do these bridges teach me about my recovery?

12. What more can I do to put the principles of this Tradition into action? How would applying this Tradition change my attitudes and actions?

IN ALL OUR AFFAIRS

13. How have I applied this Tradition outside NA? How else might the principles of this Tradition guide my thinking or my actions?

14. Where else in my life do I experience membership? Do I feel a part of or apart from?

15. Where else do I encounter requirements for membership? How willing am I to accept them or participate on their terms? What "requirements for membership" do I struggle with in other areas of my life?

16. Where else would it be appropriate to practice membership in the ways I do in NA—being of service, being a part of decisions, contributing financially, or in other ways? What else does it mean to me to practice membership outside of NA?

17. What impact has my membership in NA made on those around me?

18. What has the Third Tradition taught me about second chances, or about compassion, that might be useful elsewhere in my life?

For Groups

Tradition Three calls the group to create an atmosphere of recovery. We are responsible to ensure that meetings offer hope to any addict. Addicts seek help in many places; what sets NA apart from many others is the power of one addict freely helping another. When we recognize the pain in another addict's eyes, we make an effort to reach out.

Membership is the right of any addict with a desire to stop using, but there is no reason someone would know that when they get here. It's up to us to explain what NA is, what it means to be a member, and how NA has helped us. In order to explain those things, we need to understand them ourselves. NA literature, including *For the Newcomer* and *An Introduction to NA Meetings,* can help us put our experience into words.

It is worth a group's time to consider what information is important and how to share it clearly and consistently. The principles are the same throughout Narcotics Anonymous, but each community, and each group, has distinct ways of doing things. That variety reflects our autonomy and creativity. Groups may explain basics in their announcements. Sometimes lists of suggestions are read or printed on meeting schedules. Some groups make it a priority to ensure that the newcomer receives literature or phone numbers. Some groups ask members to raise their hands if they are willing to sponsor. There is no one right way, and each group seeks its own solutions.

Creating community includes building bridges and establishing and maintaining boundaries. Our Third Tradition tells us that we do have a requirement for membership: We must have a desire to stop using. Still, it's not for anyone else to say whether we qualify. Our desire to ensure that everything is just right can sometimes lead us to the letter rather than the spirit of our Traditions. Every addict should be able to feel safe and welcome at every NA meeting. That is the atmosphere of recovery our Traditions foster and protect.

Tradition Three reminds us of that spirit: the warm welcome, respect, and empathy that make NA feel like home. Care for the newcomer is a sacred trust. No matter what is going on in our own lives, sharing with a suffering addict is an opportunity to get outside ourselves. Empathy creates identification and offers gratitude and perspective.

One of the deepest challenges for groups is to remain open to all and still create a safe, hospitable atmosphere. Group unity and a powerful sense of community can protect us from the challenges that come with open membership. A strong NA message, clear boundaries, a loving Higher Power, and unity can protect us from ourselves and from many ills of the societies around us. We do our best to safeguard those who are vulnerable without making others feel unwelcome.

Some people come to NA to do harm, sell drugs, or engage in other destructive activity. Groups may struggle with predatory, exploitative, inappropriate, or violent behavior. There are times when action is necessary to protect members from danger, but when problems are resolved without crisis or disrespect, NA demonstrates its difference from the places we came from. Finding peaceful ways to help all addicts to recover in dignity carries a powerful message. We gain little by ignoring difficulties, and stand to lose much if we avoid the challenges we face. The group can seek solutions before reacting and creating more problems. Just like in our own lives, we can't solve a problem until we identify our part. The service pamphlet *Disruptive and Violent Behavior*, the *PR Handbook*, and members who have been through similar challenges can help us protect the group and all its members.

Groups can't refuse an addict membership, but sometimes our actions or attitudes push people out. A member shared, "When our marriage broke up, I resented anyone who was nice to my ex. I said I wanted the best for her, I prayed for her sometimes, but then I'd stalk social media and get mad at my friends who were still friends with her." This kind of drama can be dismissed as foolishness, but when our actions are inconsistent with our principles, it affects the group as well as our personal recovery. Making space for each other to recover can sometimes challenge us, but the rewards are great for all involved. We practice these principles because they are essential to our freedom from active addiction. The simple respect we show when we allow an addict to recover in dignity, even if we find them attractive or have history with them, may be a spiritual gift beyond measure.

Sometimes physical barriers can get in the way of a welcoming atmosphere. We may not notice the accessibility of our meeting space, for example, until an addict with additional needs tries to attend. Our informational pamphlet *Accessibility for Those with Additional Needs* offers guidance on how to ensure that all addicts can make their way into meetings and find a message of hope. We follow the guidance of Tradition Three, considering whether our meetings are welcoming to all addicts in our community.

Seeing addicts at different ages and cleantimes, from different communities, cultures, faiths, and backgrounds, tells each of us that there is room in NA for all of us. Sometimes groups have to work a little harder to ensure that a newcomer who doesn't seem to fit in can feel welcome. "When I walked into my first meeting, there was no one there who looked like me, but the group welcomed me and encouraged me to stay," one member shared. "I made sure to stay so that the next newcomer who looked like me would feel like they could stay, too." It may be useful to have a conversation about how the group can be more inclusive, but sometimes the question of "who's missing from our meetings" is one we can't easily answer ourselves. We can assess how welcoming we are if we pay attention to whether newcomers come back.

When we make a decision to join a home group, we might not know that we are about to fall in love. Still, much of the time, that's what happens. We take pride in our group, and are glad to see people recover in the atmosphere we help create. We come to love our group, the members in it, and the place we meet. Our willingness to act in a spirit of unity and service opens the door for all addicts who care to join us.

GROUP INVENTORY QUESTIONS _____

The questions below offer ways to begin—or continue—group inventory or discussion focused on this Tradition.

1. What does an atmosphere of recovery feel like? Why is it so important that we generate an atmosphere of recovery?

2. How do we carry a message that is both clear and welcoming? How can we help newcomers understand our message?

3. How can our group communicate what it means to be a member? How do we support those who have yet to make their decision about membership?

4. Who is missing from our meetings? Is there something our group can do to better provide a welcoming atmosphere? Is our group accessible for those members with additional needs?

5. What is the relationship between welcoming and anonymity? Does our group welcome some addicts better than others?

6. Do we make judgments or assumptions about who will hear a message and who won't? How do those judgments get in the way of practicing Tradition Three without reservations?

7. How can we ensure that our group is a safe place? What can a group do about predatory behavior? How do we address situations where a member's presence threatens other members?

8. How can we apply the Third Tradition when challenged by disruptive members? What should we do about disruptive or offensive behavior? How does our group respond to members who share in ways that make other members uncomfortable?

9. Can a group put additional requirements on membership?

10. What is the difference between "group membership" and membership in NA as a whole?

11. Do members of our group have strong social bonds with each other? Do those bonds make the meeting feel inviting or intimidating? How can we help others feel included?

12. How does this Tradition help us understand anonymity? How does anonymity help us understand this Tradition? How do we practice anonymity in terms of this Tradition?

13. Discuss any bridges between this Tradition and other Traditions. What do these bridges teach us about our group?

14. What more can we do to bring the principles of this Tradition into our group efforts? What could we do differently to better fulfill our primary purpose?

In Service

Everywhere that addicts suffer, our message is the same: An addict, any addict, can stop using drugs, lose the desire to use, and find a new way to live. There is a clear connection between the Third Tradition and the Fifth. We want all addicts to feel welcome, and we want to do our best to carry the message. Our task in service is to ensure that addicts have the opportunity to recover in Narcotics Anonymous. The Third Tradition reminds us of that "any addict" in our message. We work to ensure that NA recovery is available to us all. Tradition Three asks us to return again and again to the question, "Who is missing?" and reminds us that every addict with a desire to stop using is important to us.

Our service bodies carry the message to addicts in our communities, even if they cannot come to us. H&I carries our message into hospitals and institutions of all types, from homeless shelters to treatment centers to penitentiaries. H&I, outreach, or concerned members may bring meetings to homebound or ill members in hospitals and care facilities. Through public information or public relations, we give presentations to professionals, from correctional officers working with incarcerated addicts to doctors whose patients may be addicted. We maintain meeting schedules, phonelines, and websites so that addicts seeking recovery can find us. To ensure that our only requirement for membership is a desire to stop using, our services continually reach out to places where addicts are seeking help. It isn't always easy, but it's our responsibility.

There is always more to do toward making NA membership available and accessible. We don't have the power to determine who will stay clean, but we do have some ability to determine who will hear our message and how they will be welcomed. Sometimes the missing addicts are those who don't speak the dominant language in the community; in other places, women or addicts of different social classes might have a hard time feeling at home in NA. We may simply identify a blank space on a map where there aren't any meetings yet. Whatever the gaps, whoever we're not yet reaching, there is always more we can do to carry our message and make recovery available.

We don't need a title to make a difference in Narcotics Anonymous. Whether we are putting away chairs or distributing meeting lists, serving on a committee or giving an addict a ride to a meeting, there is always more to do. NA members all have an opportunity and a responsibility to serve, but that doesn't mean we serve in any position, any time. As members we are all equal, but that doesn't mean that we are all qualified or eligible for the same service positions at the same time. Some members are better at talking to newcomers, and some are good at getting the literature distributed or the bills paid.

Our Fourth Concept suggests that leadership qualities be carefully considered when choosing trusted servants; we know these are not the only qualities that matter. Finding where we can be most effective in service is rewarding, and so is service that presents a steep learning curve. Service bodies have a responsibility to see that the member assuming a service position has the skills and support to rise to the challenge in a manner that will be best for everyone—most especially the still-suffering addict.

When we select trusted servants, our primary purpose, rather than favoritism, should be our guide. Our job is to do our best to ensure that the member is right for the position, and the position is right for the member. When we do, it benefits both the member who serves and NA as a whole. Service bodies shouldn't run popularity contests, keep service positions within a sponsorship family, or exclude members who may challenge the consensus. A service body may fill a service position, or leave it vacant, because it is in the best interest of NA as a whole. Decisions about who serves should always be based in our commitment to carrying the message.

Tradition Three does not mean we can behave however we want in a meeting, and it does not mean we can do whatever we like in service with no accountability. When disagreements arise, when we are obliged to set limits or follow through on guidelines, we still have a responsibility to treat each other with respect and to address problems with care. Every NA member has a right to recover in dignity and be treated as an equal. In the same spirit, our trusted servants have a right to serve and recover in an atmosphere of mutual respect, even when we disagree. The ability to keep coming back is always a life-or-death issue, and it is not our place to allow differences— or even wrongdoing—to rob any addict of membership. This is not easy. The benefits of learning to resolve conflict in a spirit of love and unity are apparent in all our relationships.

Sometimes the circumstances aren't right for us to serve. This doesn't have to be a reflection on our value as a member. In one small area, a member with many years clean had served the PR committee for most of her time in NA. She knew the job and was amazingly good at answering hard questions.

Then she got sick and had to take some pretty strong medication. She did it with the help of *In Times of Illness,* her sponsor, and NA friends, and no one questioned her recovery. The side effects were significant, though, and when she gave a panel presentation, she appeared to be impaired. The committee members understood her situation, but the audience did not and could not; it was none of their business. That day, in spite of her recovery and service experience, she was not a good spokesperson for NA. It didn't mean her service was over, but it was time for her to step back and help other members learn to present as well as she once did.

Narcotics Anonymous is much larger than it once was. Our Fellowship spans the globe, and our groups are growing in places very far from each other both geographically and culturally. Our Third Tradition makes it possible for membership to be the same for addicts in very different places, and for our message to be heard and understood in dozens of languages and cultures. One member shared, "The beauty of NA became real when I saw members at an NA event embrace and sit together when their home countries were on the brink of war." We may notice this more when we see such strong differences melt away, but it can be just as powerful to sit in a meeting or to serve with another addict with whom we've had personal conflict.

Our only requirement for membership is a desire to stop using, and our vision is that it will be possible for every one of us to find recovery in our own language and culture. We can hear NA speak to us in words we understand, and experience the freedom our program promises, no matter who we are or where we are. Tradition Three opens our program to all addicts with a desire to stop using. That allows our Fellowship to grow and develop beyond our wildest dreams.

WORKSHOP QUESTIONS

The questions below offer a way to begin—or continue—a service discussion or workshop focused on this Tradition.

1. What is the relationship between this service body and the still-suffering addict?

2. Who is missing from our meetings? How and why do outside issues affect opportunities for addicts to recover in NA in our community?

3. Are there some addicts we think we cannot reach? What reservations do we have about reaching out?

4. How does our service body help groups to reach all addicts in our community? What challenges do our groups face in practicing Tradition Three? How do we assist the groups we serve in their efforts? Is there more we can do?

5. How does this body welcome new trusted servants? What kind of support do we provide to new trusted servants? How do newcomers participate in service?

6. What are some qualifications for service beyond a desire to recover? Why are they necessary? What different kinds of opportunities to serve are available in this service body?

7. How does our own relationship to anonymity affect our ability to serve? How does our understanding of anonymity help us to accept how others serve? What consequences could arise from having our anonymity compromised?

8. How does this Tradition help us understand anonymity? How does anonymity help us understand this Tradition? How do we practice anonymity in terms of this Tradition?

9. Discuss any bridges between this Tradition and one or more of the Twelve Concepts. What do these bridges teach us about our service efforts?

10. What more can we do to bring the principles of this Tradition into our service efforts? What could we do differently to better carry out our services?

Our Third Tradition offers relief from reservations we might have about membership and about each other. We have nothing to prove, no one to impress, nothing to lose but our needless suffering, and nothing to gain but our freedom.

This simple declaration makes a commitment to unity, anonymity, and the power of the program. Making the decision to join Narcotics Anonymous is the first of many decisions we will make as a member. We who had been utterly controlled by our addiction are now free to make decisions that will save our lives—and the lives of many others.

When we make a decision to try NA, we have no idea where it will take us. Our desire starts us on a journey that can set us free from our obsession and compulsion. This decision is the beginning of a new way of life for us. Joining in fellowship with others finally frees us to be ourselves.

*Each group should be autonomous
except in matters affecting other
groups or NA as a whole.*

TRADITION

4

Recovery is an ongoing journey to freedom. When we live the NA program, we are constantly experiencing new opportunities for growth, and also discovering our limitations. As our lives improve, our responsibilities increase. Freedom becomes much more complicated, and much more beautiful.

Our experience of freedom is no longer a simple absence of boundaries. As we progress in the Steps, we see the ways addiction tied us in knots, and we start to understand how self-centeredness, fear, and resentment continue to bind us. As our vision clears, we see more and more hope on the horizon. Freedom can transform from a fantasy of doing whatever we want to the ability to live with joy and gratitude in our present reality.

We balance autonomy with responsibility. When we keep our purpose in focus, our autonomy makes more sense. The responsible practice of autonomy helps us to see our relationships and obligations more clearly and to use our creativity, our imagination, and our enthusiasm to help us fulfill our purpose—in our groups, in our lives, and in service to our Higher Power.

Having a purpose makes our freedom meaningful. We need meaning to make our autonomy constructive. The autonomy of our groups becomes a tool for recovery when we remember our primary purpose; our personal autonomy becomes much more powerful when we know our own purpose and have a sense of meaning in our lives.

Understanding and accepting ourselves is a gift of recovery. Autonomy allows us to express who we are with integrity and to carry a message: the truth of our own experience, in our own way.

Tradition Four

Our Tradition of autonomy ensures that every NA group is able to carry the message to the best of its ability. Each group makes decisions for itself and takes responsibility for those decisions. The result is that each of us is able to recover in complete creative freedom. We find ways to reach out that make sense to us, and our groups make decisions that best serve the needs of the addicts who attend.

We cannot practice one of the Traditions without the others, and the other eleven Traditions help to shape our autonomy and remind us of its limits. We carry an NA message, and we are part of a Fellowship that extends from the doors of our group through our local community and around the world. Our actions always have an effect on those around us, and we can choose at every moment what we want that to be. We can be a force for unity, providing a warm and open atmosphere for recovery. It's a decision: We can also decide to be divisive, exclusive, or rigid. But that probably won't be attractive for long, and it's unlikely to keep us clean. Because personal recovery depends on NA unity, Tradition Four asks us to consider our actions in relation to other addicts, groups, and NA as a whole.

Freedom and responsibility work hand in hand. Our groups have autonomy but are asked to attend carefully to the ways that our actions may "affect other groups or NA as a whole"—which is to say, our local NA community, the rest of the NA Fellowship, and our relationship with those outside NA. Our autonomy is precious to us, and at times we defend it fiercely. The most important thing we do with autonomy is to carry the message. Our task is to ensure that when we exercise autonomy, we do it in ways that enhance our efforts to carry the message, rather than interfere with it. Autonomy is part of a larger whole—just as we see our groups, our service bodies, and ourselves as part of something greater. This Tradition both offers freedom and establishes boundaries for us in ways specific rules or policies never could.

Self-obsession is the core of our disease, and one of the defining features of self-obsession is that we do not see the impact of our actions on the people around us—or we just don't care. In recovery, we recognize that we have an effect on the people in our lives. Through the harm we do in our addiction, and the loving assistance we offer in recovery, we can see that our actions do matter. Tradition Two teaches us about group conscience, and Tradition Four asks us to let that conscience be our guide.

In Narcotics Anonymous, we say that "our message is hope and the promise of freedom," but most of us don't come here knowing what freedom means, or what it feels like. It's a common thread in our stories: In addiction, we were seeking freedom and found ourselves imprisoned. As we experience freedom from active addiction, we start to get a better sense of what recovery means—freedom from obsession and compulsion, the joy of making our own choices, seeking our own recovery, learning who we are and what we believe. Our experience of freedom is not separate from our development of integrity.

As we mature in recovery, we learn to exercise sound judgment in how we make decisions, place our trust, and meet our responsibilities. Immaturity and unrealistic expectations are consequences of unhealthy reliance on others. When we have not had the opportunity to make decisions in our lives, we need experience to learn how to do it well. Responsible use of independent judgment develops in an atmosphere of freedom. As we make responsible decisions for ourselves, we develop our own conscience and maturity.

In our groups, we are free to carry the message in whatever way seems most effective to us. This doesn't free us from accountability to our fellows. In fact, we are asked to consider them with every decision we make: How will this affect the other groups? What could be the consequences for NA as a whole? This accountability teaches us to look; our work in the Steps helps us to see.

Tradition Three frees us from the need to judge other members, and Tradition Four frees us from the need to judge other groups. Traditions Four and Five together remind us that there are many ways to accomplish our purpose. As long as carrying the message is our first priority, our diverse methods, formats, personalities, and cultures all help us to reach addicts and to form the kinds of connections that will sustain us.

WORD BY WORD

Define, expand on, or clarify the words or phrases from this Tradition, one at a time or in relation to each other, for writing or discussion with your sponsor or other NA members.

Example: except

When a statement is true, but not about a particular case, we use the word *except*. *Except* frees us from our tendency toward absolutes. In both the Ninth Step and the Fourth Tradition, the word *except* serves to temper our good intentions before we go too far and cause harm. We learn to tell the difference between our impulses, compulsions, good ideas, and the will of our Higher Power. *Except* keeps us from backing ourselves into corners; in this Tradition, it asks us to consider others as we make decisions. It's a limit, but not a block. Within our principles we can be creative, independent, unified, and humble.

SPIRITUAL PRINCIPLES

Each Tradition embodies a variety of spiritual principles. The list of principles and values below may be useful as we consider applications of this Tradition. Explore them in writing or discussion with your sponsor or other NA members. If other principles or values not listed below seem relevant for you, include those as well.

• independence	• freedom	• responsibility	• humility
• open-mindedness	• trust	• compassion	• connection
• love	• unity	• anonymity	• selfless
• service	• commitment	• consistency	• creativity
• autonomy	• integrity		

Example: creativity

To some of us, it might seem strange to find creativity on a list of spiritual principles, but our pamphlet *Another Look* includes creative action as one of the goals of recovery, alongside freedom and goodwill. "Creative action is not a mysterious procedure," the pamphlet explains, "although it is an inside job. . . . Often, it means simply listening to those hunches and intuitive feelings that we think would benefit others or ourselves, and acting on them spontaneously."

In order to be creative, we have to let go. When we are bound by insecurity and the need to control, our attempts at creativity end in suffering and frustration. When we allow ourselves the freedom to listen to that inner voice and act on it, we are surprised by what we can do, and by what we discover within ourselves. Some of us express our creativity in art or music, but often the most creative things we can do unfold when we serve selflessly. When we experience our service as creative action, we experience ourselves as an instrument and as part of something greater. Selfless service is a form of creativity available to us all. Our action has purpose and our lives have meaning. When we admit our creativity and allow ourselves to express it, we see our Higher Power's will for us in action.

For Members

Although this Tradition clearly speaks to us about *group* autonomy, many of us find application of its principles in our own lives to be useful. Personal autonomy allows us to be ourselves, and it is precisely by being ourselves that we are best able to carry the message to another suffering addict. It's because we are so different—because our unity should never demand uniformity—that we can be true to ourselves and honest about our experience. That honesty is the most powerful tool we have in our efforts to carry the message.

In active addiction, we were only too willing to declare our autonomy, taking advantage at every turn and declaring our "freedom" in the process. Or we never aspired to personal autonomy, perhaps even finding distorted comfort in our hopeless dependence, seeing a lack of responsibility as freedom. In recovery, we come to understand the slavery we mistook for freedom, and our recovery is a progressive process of freeing ourselves from the bonds of addiction.

Gaining freedom in recovery does not mean we don't have responsibilities. The types of obligations we have in our lives will differ depending on the relationships we have and the roles we play in those relationships. In jobs, in service, in our communities and families, our actions have an impact on others. How do our actions affect Narcotics Anonymous? How do they affect our families, our friends, our coworkers, and our communities? We start to understand that we are not alone—we live in connection with others even when we don't feel particularly connected, and our actions matter.

Personal autonomy does not have the same value to all of us. In fact, it may have been a long time since some of us made any decisions for ourselves. Some of us have been institutionalized; others of us stayed dependent on family. Some of us found ourselves in relationships or organizations where our autonomy was curtailed. Making the simplest decisions for ourselves can be challenging, and we may seek out someone or something that will make decisions for us. In our personal lives, autonomy looks a lot like self-determination: We practice using the tools our spiritual principles provide to begin shaping a life we can accept. Even when there are severe limits on our physical abilities or on our liberty, we can experience freedom. An elderly member adapting to physical limitations defined freedom as "the ability to love unencumbered by fear." When we are able to view freedom as a spiritual condition, we can be less driven to test its limits and more open to exploring the enormous possibilities it offers us.

QUESTIONS FOR MEMBERS _____

The questions below offer a way to begin—or continue—the process of writing, reflection, and discussion of this Tradition with your sponsor or other NA members.

IN NA

1. What is the difference between personal autonomy, my will, and self-will?

2. How do I practice autonomy as a member of the NA Fellowship? What does autonomy mean to me in the context of my personal recovery? In NA service?

3. What is the relationship between my personal autonomy and our common welfare? How do I strike a balance between my wants and needs and the good of the whole?

4. How can I exercise personal autonomy in a way that benefits our common welfare? In what ways could my choices seem to compromise my relationship with NA? How can I reconcile my personal autonomy and my fear of being judged?

5. How does this Tradition help me understand anonymity? How does anonymity help me understand this Tradition? Do I practice anonymity in terms of this Tradition?

6. Describe any bridges between this Tradition and one or more of the Twelve Steps. What do these bridges teach me about my recovery?

7. What more can I do to put the principles of this Tradition into action? How would applying this Tradition change my attitudes and actions?

IN ALL OUR AFFAIRS

8. How have I applied this Tradition outside NA? How else might the principles of this Tradition guide my thinking or my actions?

9. What is my understanding of the relationship between autonomy and goodwill?

10. What challenges do I experience in allowing myself and others to have autonomy?

11. How do I balance independence and responsibility?

12. How does my integrity impact my freedom?

13. What are similarities and differences between freedom and autonomy?

14. How does defiance distort my perception of autonomy?

15. How do I exercise autonomy in the context of my personal relationships? My work relationships? In service to my community or other organizations?

For Groups

This Tradition addresses itself to our groups, and it is important that we maintain that focus as we explore other applications of its principles. Tradition Four tells us, "Each group should be autonomous except in matters affecting other groups or NA as a whole." The words *should be* imply that this is a goal rather than an absolute. Sometimes a group may accept assistance and support from other groups or from NA service bodies. There are times when a local community steps in to support a struggling group for a good reason. For example, established groups occasionally sponsor or support groups that are geographically isolated or that meet particular needs. In these cases, it's helpful to consider carefully the nature of such help and to set some goals to help the group achieve full autonomy and self-support.

While addiction and recovery are common bonds we all share, in some ways we are very different. Some of our differences are obvious, and some less so; some of our differences have much more meaning in the outside world than in NA. Still, they affect the ways we see and experience our relationships with each other. Autonomy means that our groups can shape themselves to be attractive in whatever way they see fit, as long as the primary purpose is to carry the message to the addict who still suffers.

There are six points based on our Traditions listed in *The Group Booklet* to help us understand our bottom lines for what constitutes a group:

- All members of a group are drug addicts, and all drug addicts are eligible for membership.

- As a group, they are self-supporting.

- As a group, their single goal is to help drug addicts recover through application of the Twelve Steps of Narcotics Anonymous.

- As a group, they have no affiliation outside of Narcotics Anonymous.

- As a group, they express no opinion on outside issues.

- As a group, their public relations policy is based on attraction rather than promotion.

Even considering these six points, each group has a lot of freedom to find ways to fulfill the primary purpose that suit the collective conscience of the group. None of our Traditions stands alone. A good test of whether an issue or decision "affects other groups or NA as a whole" is to consider carefully whether our decision is consistent with the guidance offered by our other Traditions. As an example, the desire to support fellow members with a common need may inspire us to create a specialized meeting format. We must remember that the Sixth Tradition cautions against endorsements and affiliation and that the Tenth Tradition warns about the dangers of expressing opinions on outside issues. We could not create a meeting format directed at addicts with particular religious or philosophical views, or a group meant for NA members who are also part of another organization outside of NA, or a group that reads material other than NA literature. Doing so would step beyond the autonomy afforded by Tradition Four by endorsing or affiliating with those outside groups, interests, or beliefs. Autonomy offers us the freedom to try new things, and we demonstrate courage when we make new efforts to better carry our message. Seeking guidance from the other eleven Traditions when we try new things allows us to do so without compromising our principles.

NA is very different from place to place. Within some NA communities, meetings are very similar to each other; other communities have a lot of diversity in their formats and styles. It can sometimes be difficult for members to distinguish between our Traditions—the guidelines that keep us alive and free—and our local customs. This is especially true when those local customs are repeated at every meeting. This may be as simple as the way we close the meeting, or as complicated as suggestions or announcements that are uniform across a region. We may be surprised to go to a new place and find that meetings can operate so differently—and still work.

Although local NA customs may make the Fellowship more or less attractive to us, we want to carefully consider decisions to change them. When we make a decision to do something differently, we should do so for a reason. Our efforts should be aimed at helping addicts pay more attention to the message if we present it differently, rather than seeking attention for ourselves.

Our groups, our neighboring communities, and our Fellowship as a whole are joined together in unity. The connections from one to the next, like strands of a spider web, are so fine they may go unseen, but they are also strong and flexible. Those connections are our shared principles, and when we make good use of those principles in our exercise of autonomy, we can be sure that we are strengthening NA as a whole.

GROUP INVENTORY QUESTIONS _____

The questions below offer ways to begin—or continue—group inventory or discussion focused on this Tradition.

1. How does creative freedom benefit NA groups? Narcotics Anonymous as a whole?

2. As groups, how do we know what affects other groups? How do our group decisions affect the Fellowship as a whole?

3. What is the importance of communication in group conscience? How do we maintain lines of communication and awareness of the needs of NA as a whole?

4. How are our group's efforts to express personality directly related to carrying the message? Do we ever try to be different for the sake of being different?

5. How can we exercise group autonomy in a way that contributes to NA unity?

6. When could our exercise of autonomy have a negative effect on other groups or NA as a whole?

7. NA service bodies are directly responsible to the NA groups; keeping autonomy in mind, what responsibilities or obligations do NA groups have to NA service bodies?

8. Why is the image of NA so important in the community? What part does each group play in the overall reputation of NA as a whole? How does our group contribute to public perceptions?

9. How does this Tradition help us understand anonymity? How does anonymity help us understand this Tradition? How do we practice anonymity in terms of this Tradition?

10. Discuss any bridges between this Tradition and other Traditions. What do these bridges teach us about our group?

11. What more can we do to bring the principles of this Tradition into our group efforts? What could we do differently to better fulfill our primary purpose?

In Service

It is critical for us to remember that, although our groups are autonomous, our service bodies are not. Our Concepts remind groups to delegate the authority necessary for services to operate, but they also remind us that final authority always rests with the groups. This doesn't mean that Tradition Four has no meaning for service bodies. There are at least two critical ways service bodies need to consider this Tradition, and they are very different.

The first is perhaps the most important: All our services exist in order to help the groups carry the message. It can be easy to forget that responsibility when we get caught up in issues or serve in a way that seems removed from the groups. Are we helping our groups to be autonomous, or are we fostering an atmosphere of dependency or obedience? Do the groups answer to their service bodies, or is it the other way around? In service, as in our personal recovery, we can be in deep trouble when we start thinking we know best. We help our groups when we do the work that might otherwise distract them from their primary purpose. We help our groups when we communicate effectively, when we support groups in sharing experience and tools for how to serve well. In service, we listen well by listening for common ground rather than for ways to prove that our idea is better. We serve our groups best when our service is sane, selfless, and simple; ego, controversy, and disunity anywhere in our community affect the atmosphere of recovery in our groups.

Although our service bodies are not autonomous, they do a lot of work—and frequently make decisions—away from the groups that authorize them. This is a second way service bodies may apply this Tradition: to carefully consider the ways in which actions affect the groups and NA as a whole. We may want to adapt some of the same questions we ask in our groups to our service bodies: Are the decisions we are making, or the actions we are taking, affecting other groups or NA as a whole? Is this a conversation we should take to our local community? Concept Eight reminds us that our services depend "on the integrity and effectiveness of our communications," and communication means more than simple reporting back and forth. Having open and frank discussions together as a community about the matters facing our service committees can help us avoid the controversy that often follows when we take action first and then seek guidance later.

Considering the impact of our decisions on others, especially on the groups we serve, allows us to be responsible in thinking through which decisions belong in the committee and which merit broader discussion. Service bodies that don't have a lot of direct involvement with the groups, such as public relations, convention committees, or local translations committees, may not always recognize the importance of open communication in building consensus beyond the limits of the committee. A decision to go forward with a bus poster campaign in one town led to meetings being overwhelmed and unprepared to handle so many newcomers. Another community coordinated newcomer workshops together with their outreach efforts and were able to support the groups, rather than overwhelming them. Convention committee decisions to change prices or location may make perfect sense within the committee, but the decision can feel heavy-handed or exclusionary if not discussed more broadly with the community beforehand.

In service bodies, Tradition Four walks hand in hand with Tradition One: How are our actions supporting unity, how are we supporting the groups, and how might we do better at fostering unity and finding consensus?

Tradition Four asks us to look for the limits to what we should do on our own, and to consider carefully when enthusiasm starts to give way to self-will. Group autonomy has made it possible for the NA program to transcend countless language and cultural barriers to help addicts find recovery. Our service bodies may be afforded trust by the groups they serve, allowing them to be flexible and adapt to the needs of each community, but that trust is not the same as autonomy.

WORKSHOP QUESTIONS

The questions below offer a way to begin—or continue—a service discussion or workshop focused on this Tradition.

1. What is the importance of creative freedom in Narcotics Anonymous groups? How can we be a resource to the groups in their expression of autonomy and creative freedom?

2. What are some of the differences in how autonomy and Tradition Four apply to groups and service bodies?

3. How does our service body learn what's important to the groups in our community? How do we include our groups in planning for local services? Do we include all the voices within our community?

4. How do our service efforts honor the needs and wishes of the groups we serve? How does our service body ensure that our decisions and actions respond to local needs? How does humility help us to serve effectively?

5. How do our recent decisions affect our local groups? Are there decisions we're making now that affect our local groups?

6. What part does effective communication play in our service efforts? What works in our local NA community as effective communication, and what doesn't? How can our communication be more effective?

7. In what ways do we address issues that affect NA as a whole? How do we determine whether our actions affect neighboring service bodies? What are our responsibilities as part of a worldwide Fellowship?

8. Do our events compete with other events in neighboring places? Is the number of events, activities, and conventions in our community too high, too low, or just right?

9. How does this Tradition help us understand anonymity? How does anonymity help us understand this Tradition? How do we practice anonymity in terms of this Tradition?

10. Discuss any bridges between this Tradition and one or more of the Twelve Concepts. What do these bridges teach us about our service efforts?

11. What more can we do to bring the principles of this Tradition into our service efforts? What could we do differently to better carry out our services?

Autonomy—the ability to make decisions for ourselves—is part of what we aspire to in recovery. Understanding what autonomy means when we are part of a larger Fellowship can help us understand the relationships between our powerlessness and our responsibility, between our actions and the people around us, between our group and the Fellowship we all share.

Tradition Four frees us from the need to regulate the behavior of others even as it challenges us to look carefully at the consequences of our own. Our open membership policy described in Tradition Three and the autonomy of our groups outlined in Tradition Four create the conditions for us to practice Tradition Five—to carry the message to the addict who still suffers, in whatever way allows us to be honest, hopeful, and humble. Anonymity reminds us that in Narcotics Anonymous we are equals, sharing our experience, strength, and hope. We do not direct, enforce, or govern; each of us carries the message in the way best suited to us, and together we create groups, services, community, and local customs, with responsibility and creative freedom.

*Each group has but one primary purpose—
to carry the message
to the addict who still suffers.*

TRADITION

In active addiction, we worked hard to reach goals that left us feeling empty, lost, and dead inside. We got what we needed, no matter the cost to ourselves or those around us. As obsession and compulsion drove us to bitter ends, we surprised ourselves at what we would do, or what we would sacrifice. The more we pursued our goals, the less we felt any sense of purpose at all.

The Fifth Tradition restores purpose to our lives: carrying a simple message to suffering addicts. In service to that purpose, we reach out. We start and support meetings. We walk our talk, work Steps, sponsor, care, and share. Our passion for recovery is a constant source of gratitude. When one addict gets clean, we don't stop. We keep reaching out. When a hundred, or a thousand, or ten thousand addicts get clean, we don't stop. There's always an addict who's dying to hear the NA message.

Narcotics Anonymous has grown from a dream to a worldwide Fellowship because so many members, inspired by a sense of purpose, have given freely to make recovery a reality all over the world. Our hope grows as we see the program in action. Our willingness grows as we see and experience the miracle of recovery in all its extraordinary diversity.

Instead of chasing empty goals, today we are driven by a sense of purpose. Gratitude in action is an engine for change: As we carry the message, our own lives transform.

Tradition Five

Our message is the heart of Narcotics Anonymous. Everything we do, everything that matters to us as a Fellowship, comes back to our simple message of hope and freedom: that an addict, any addict, can stop using drugs, lose the desire to use, and find a new way of life. No one is too sick or too well, too rich or too poor, too far gone or too far away to qualify. It is available to us all.

Carrying the message is what matters. We see it in our meetings, when an empty room is transformed into an atmosphere of warmth and empathy. We see it when members generously give of their time and themselves to serve. We see it when we set aside our personal differences or interests to reach out to a suffering addict. Many of us, in moments of distress, have been told to go help somebody. Reaching out breaks the bonds of self-obsession and frees us to see ourselves and our world from a new perspective. In our hope for each other, we find hope for ourselves.

So many of us were seeking freedom when we started using. We were looking for a way out of our feelings, our responsibilities, and our lives. The freedom we find in NA is different from that. The Twelve Steps bring us freedom from obsessive thought and compulsive action. Our Fellowship brings us freedom from isolation. We are free to become exactly who we are and to find a sense of fulfillment in our lives, whatever that means for us. We are set free to love and to care, to hope and to hurt, to reach out and to grow no matter where we are in our recovery. The ability to grow spiritually enables us to find freedom, even within the walls of a cell. Our greatest freedom is not outside ourselves but within.

That hope and freedom drive us through our brightest days and our darkest suffering. Staying connected reminds us that there is always more to be done—and always more being done. We often speak of the addict with two days clean telling the addict with one day clean, "It works." As we stay clean, we also have the experience of the addict with two days clean showing the addict with ten years clean that it works. We never know where our message of hope will come from. Keeping our purpose primary allows us all to carry the message, and gives each of us the ability to hear it.

Our unity is possible because our message is clear. We are not confused about why we are here, and we can set our differences aside and do that one thing. Our Traditions help us see what is important, and some of the ways we lose sight of that. Many of us have found additional rewards from places outside the rooms of NA, but none of that is what we come to NA to share. We are here to share the simple truth about our recovery in Narcotics Anonymous. The Steps help us to peel away the lies and pain that distract us from the truth. When our meetings are honest and true, when the atmosphere of recovery in our group is safe and welcoming, when every addict who comes in the door is met with dignity and empathy, our message is more powerful than words.

 ## WORD BY WORD

Define, expand on, or clarify the words or phrases from this Tradition, one at a time or in relation to each other, for writing or discussion with your sponsor or other NA members.

Example: primary

One way to think about the word *primary* is "most important." The most important task of a group is to carry the message to the addict who still suffers. Our group may serve other purposes for us: a place we find support, where we go to see our friends, or where we just feel safe from insanity for a little while. Our group may serve other purposes, as well. It may serve as a literature study or a place of celebration; it may reach into a part of the community no other meeting does. No matter what secondary purposes a group may serve, its *primary* purpose is to carry the message.

Another way to understand *primary* is in terms of "primary colors"—they do not reduce to any other color; they are pure. Around the world and around town we experience many different kinds of NA meetings, but what's always the same is our simple message, pure and true. Our diversity strengthens and affirms the reality of our simple message. Across all of our differences, the same simple program works. There is hope for us all in Narcotics Anonymous.

SPIRITUAL PRINCIPLES

Each Tradition embodies a variety of spiritual principles. The list of principles and values below may be useful as we consider applications of this Tradition. Explore them in writing or discussion with your sponsor or other NA members. If other principles or values not listed below seem relevant for you, include those as well.

- integrity
- commitment
- open-mindedness
- vigilance
- hope

- responsibility
- empathy
- surrender
- passion

- unity
- service
- fidelity
- compassion

- anonymity
- purpose
- consistency
- security

Example: consistency

Consistency is a spiritual principle that keeps us doing what we do. It begins with the refrain, "Keep coming back!" Coming to meetings regularly helps us stay clean, and it also carries a message of hope: We keep coming back because it works. The group depends on its members, and members depend on the group being true to its purpose. Showing up consistently, sharing honestly, and treating others with respect all further our primary purpose. A consistent message is powerful. When our actions and message are clear and consistent, our groups cannot fail.

For Members

The recovering addict and the group need each other to survive. The group depends on the selfless service of its members, and members depend on the group being true to its purpose. The Fifth Tradition is bound up with the First: Our personal recovery depends on NA unity, and our unity depends on our attention to our primary purpose.

We don't have to be on Step Twelve to carry a message of recovery, but working the Steps helps us to understand our message. When we struggle to articulate a clear message, individually or as a group, we can look to our foundation in the Steps to help us understand. The First Step of Narcotics Anonymous is unique. Rather than addressing a single symptom or substance, we admit our powerlessness over the disease that drives us. It's this Step that allows us to recover together without concern for "what or how much you used." Recovery is an inside job, because addiction is an inside disease.

The expansiveness of this First Step sometimes leads to confusion: It can seem like anyone with any obsession might find themselves in NA. Although our First Step is so broad, our literature is clear: Very simply, an addict is a man or woman whose life is controlled by drugs. We don't need to overthink our message or wear ourselves out trying to decide who belongs here. When our message is clear, it is attractive to addicts. We find each other.

When we come to this Tradition as individual members, our first task is to consider our personal role in helping each group to fulfill its primary purpose. When we live the program, read the literature, listen to the readings, practice these principles, and apply our Traditions, we really don't have to worry too much about our message. Our recovery will speak for itself. Each of us carries a message. We are always examples of recovery in action, whether we mean to be or not. People look to our actions to understand how Narcotics Anonymous works. We pay attention to our own relationship to the addict who still suffers: Do we welcome newcomers at our meetings? Are we respectful and compassionate? Are we providing the new member with a safe place to recover? When an addict seeks recovery in NA, we have an obligation to reach out.

Being part of a Fellowship that is clear and passionate about its purpose can give us a sense of what it means to be clear and passionate in our own lives. When we come to understand what it means for our group to have a purpose, we may want to ask ourselves about our own primary purpose.

Many of us find a bridge between Tradition Five and Step Eleven: When we pray for an understanding of a Higher Power's will for us and the power to carry that out, we are seeking a higher purpose as well. For some of us, taking on the primary purpose of NA can become a life's work: Carrying the message will always be where we find our deepest rewards. Others of us find our greatest passion elsewhere: in our families, our careers, our creativity, or our faith. Whether we find that sense of connection through one outlet or many, being driven or called to a purpose can be one of the most joyful experiences in life.

Over the years we may experience a number of different callings or get excited about different directions we can take. Our belief about where we are directed, however, may not determine what happens. When our lives change unexpectedly, we can have deep doubts about ourselves and the path we are on. Going through those shifts can change more than our direction; they help to shape our faith and deepen our surrender.

There are times when we need a restoration to hope, just as we need a restoration to sanity. The two may be closely related. Sometimes we can borrow someone else's faith when ours is lacking; sometimes our empathy carries us through. Even when we don't have much hope for ourselves, we can still get excited for the member picking up a keytag or a medallion, or the addict experiencing new freedom in recovery. As we experience surprise, joy, and sometimes bitter disappointment, we learn the difference between hope and fantasy. Hope becomes more solid and more secure than our passing wishes or expectations.

There is such a strong connection between Tradition Five and Step Twelve that we can almost see them as singular and plural of the same idea. The group is able to serve its purpose because its members are willing to make a commitment to serve—to try to carry the message in whatever way we can. Step Twelve suggests that this is a result of a spiritual awakening, but the action of carrying the message also wakes us up. The spiritual awakening we experience when we reach out to another addict is unlike anything we have felt before.

Empathy and connection are the beginning. We start to see our experience as a resource. Everything we go through can become a tool to help someone who is suffering. We may gain wisdom, or we may simply be able to say, "I went through that, and I stayed clean." We experience a powerful connection when we hear someone tell our story or share something about themselves that we had guarded as a deep secret. Our work carrying the message means that no pain is wasted. When we are able to use our own suffering to help another addict get through a day clean, we start to feel that sense of purpose in our lives that we see in our groups. Our stories are keys to freedom. The door we open swings both ways: We free ourselves in the moment we reach out to help someone else.

We get the message as we carry the message; we find a purpose when we serve a purpose. When our purpose is clear, our passion for recovery carries us through. When we lose our own way, the strong sense of purpose in NA reminds us who we are, how far we have come, and how much is still available to us all.

QUESTIONS FOR MEMBERS _____

The questions below offer a way to begin—or continue—the process of writing, reflection, and discussion of this Tradition with your sponsor or other NA members.

IN NA

1. How did I first hear the message of NA? What helped me to hear it?

2. How does our primary purpose in NA relate to my own purpose for coming to meetings and for being in recovery?

3. As a member, what is the message that I carry? What does it mean to me to carry a clear NA message?

4. How did I understand freedom from active addiction when I was new? How do I understand it today? If our message is hope and the promise of freedom, what is my hope today?

5. How does Tradition Five influence what I say and do at meetings? What message does my behavior carry?

6. When I share, how do I connect my experience with the overall message of NA? With the topic of the meeting?

7. Do I hesitate to share my own challenges and struggles? How do I feel when a more experienced member shares about ongoing difficulties and struggles?

8. How am I most effective when carrying the message? What can I do that I'm not already doing? How might I expand my ability to carry the message?

9. When do my opinions or feelings get in the way of carrying a message or in the way of hearing the message? Is there a particular addict I need to find compassion for?

10. Do my personal beliefs get mixed in with the message I carry? Does my NA message get mixed up with my personal beliefs?

11. What is an atmosphere of recovery? As a member of an NA group, what am I doing to create and sustain an atmosphere of recovery?

12. What do I recognize as exploitative behavior? What is my part in our shared responsibility to keep NA a safe place for all?

13. In what ways can I best carry the NA message? What is my experience with doing a Twelfth Step call? What message do I carry as a sponsor and as a sponsee? What does the saying "carry the message, not the addict" mean to me?

14. How does this Tradition help me understand anonymity? How does anonymity help me understand this Tradition? How do I practice anonymity in terms of this Tradition?

15. Describe any bridges between this Tradition and one or more of the Twelve Steps. What do these bridges teach me about my recovery?

16. What more can I do to put the principles of this Tradition into action? How would applying this Tradition change my attitudes and actions?

IN ALL OUR AFFAIRS

17. How have I applied this Tradition outside NA? How else might the principles of this Tradition guide my thinking or my actions?

18. How does my primary purpose vary in different parts of my life? How does a sense of purpose help me to set and understand my priorities? How does purpose guide my actions? What is the difference between purpose and desire?

19. Do my varying purposes lead me to carry particular messages? What are they? When and where do I carry them? How does the practice of carrying a clear message in NA help me in other areas of my life?

20. Does my sense of purpose change over time? How have changes in my values, priorities, or roles affected my purpose? What do I do when my priorities seem to be in conflict?

21. What helps determine my sense of purpose? When circumstances set priorities for me, does my sense of myself change? How do I practice integrity when life circumstances shape my priorities?

For Groups

We often talk about our message in very broad terms—hope, freedom, finding a new way of life. However, our experience of getting the message often happens in very small ways. Someone shares like they were reading our mind; some members ask us to join them for coffee after the meeting; someone reaches out and gives us a hug, or offers us a chair, or notices that we're new and asks our name. Most often the experience of "getting the message" is all tangled up with feeling welcome, feeling safe, feeling like we belong, and beginning to think of ourselves as members.

Our actions are more important than our words. The actions that make an addict feel included, cared about, and "a part of" are among the most powerful ways we carry the NA message, whether we're reaching out to the brand-newcomer, the middle-timer, or the longest-timer in the room. We are never too old for a message of hope. Welcome and concern almost always feel good, whether we are new or not. Our members carry the message in our groups, and our groups work best when everyone feels welcome to be a member.

The power of the NA group springs from its focus on our primary purpose, and the power of our message comes through the unity and cohesion of our groups. The group is the most effective means of carrying the message, but it can't do that without caring and committed members. A group carries the message by creating an atmosphere of recovery. In the group, addicts come together to share before, during, and after the meeting. In any given meeting, members are at different stages in their recovery, experience different levels of desire, and seek different levels of growth. The variety of honest sharing in the meeting, as much as what any one addict says, helps us identify. When other addicts are willing to get vulnerable and share, it makes it easier for each of us to do the same.

If a meeting is not serving a need, it generally goes away. It's important to notice when groups are growing or shrinking, or when and why groups struggle with self-support or finding trusted servants. Is the group attractive to other addicts? In a place where people have their choice of meetings, there may be a reason why a struggling meeting isn't getting chosen. A group inventory may help to determine whether changes are needed to help the meeting carry the message more effectively or whether it's time to let it go.

On the other hand, patience and humility may be necessary for a group to take root. Quite a few NA communities got their start due to the persistence of one or two members who kept showing up to open the doors, even when it seemed that no one would ever join them. "I sat in the only NA meeting in town by myself for two years, reading from the White Booklet. When someone finally walked in and asked if this was the NA meeting, I almost didn't know what to say. I just said, 'Welcome.'"

Size is not the only measure of a meeting's success. Small meetings can be intimate, unified, and solid; they can provide a safe and steady place to share and to call home. A meeting can be just right with ten people or two hundred; the question is always about the atmosphere of recovery. Are people coming back? Are newcomers staying? Are people sharing honestly and openly? Is the message clear?

A group can be diverted from our primary purpose by a variety of things. It can be more invested in its social life than in the message; it can get bogged down in controversy or NA business; it can allow ego, power, or personalities to become more important than the message. There is a simple way to recognize when a meeting stops serving its purpose: Addicts stop coming back. Popularity is not the measure of spiritual health, but when a meeting dwindles noticeably, when the cohesion of the group weakens, when addicts feel physically or emotionally unsafe, when members no longer care to serve or resentments start to infiltrate the meeting, we can usually look to the group's priorities to understand. Just as in our personal recovery, each new day brings a chance to start fresh. At any moment, our group can stop, consider its priorities, and ensure our focus is squarely on carrying a message of recovery.

Magic happens in NA meetings. We hear the music of the message even when we don't understand the language in which it is shared. Our groups host meetings and sometimes events, but more than that they become communities themselves. The bond we share with our fellow group members can be deep and loving, growing over years into something a lot like family. When we focus on our primary purpose, our groups grow into something greater than the sum of their parts. A shared sense of purpose creates its own bond, and as we nurture that purpose the connections between us grow solid and loving.

GROUP INVENTORY QUESTIONS _____

The questions below offer ways to begin—or continue—group inventory or discussion focused on this Tradition.

1. Why does a group need a purpose? Why is it so important that we keep our meetings focused on our primary purpose? How does focusing on our primary purpose shape the atmosphere of recovery in our group?

2. Which of our group's practices or customs relate to the Fifth Tradition? How do we maintain a focus on NA's primary purpose?

3. How does our group ensure it is a safe and welcome place? What can we do to make all members feel more welcome? What can our group do to address behavior that challenges our primary purpose?

4. What do we value most about our home group? What part does our group's diversity or sense of identity play in reaching those who attend our meetings? How does our group distinctively carry out our primary purpose? What other purposes does our group serve?

5. What is the message that we carry as a group? How does our group attract addicts or carry a message? How do our business meetings help us? What is the role of the group in carrying a clear message?

6. How and why did this group get started? Has the atmosphere of recovery in our meetings increased or diminished recently? Is there anything we need to do differently? What are the ways our format helps or hinders our ability to carry the message?

7. What is our group's responsibility to still-suffering addicts? How do we carry the message to the addicts who have not found our meeting? How can we make our meetings more accessible?

8. What is the importance of a clear NA message? How does our group foster understanding of our Steps and Traditions? How do we help our members understand Narcotics Anonymous?

9. Does this group make space for all addicts to hear the message? Is the message we're carrying reaching everyone in the room?

10. How does this Tradition help us understand anonymity? How does anonymity help us understand this Tradition? How do we practice anonymity in terms of this Tradition?

11. Discuss any bridges between this Tradition and other Traditions. What do these bridges teach us about our group?

12. What more can we do to bring the principles of this Tradition into our group efforts? What could we do differently to better fulfill our primary purpose?

In Service

NA service is varied and creative. We do all kinds of work to carry the message and support our groups. We bring meetings or panels into hospitals and institutions, and make presentations to inform providers and the public about Narcotics Anonymous; we hold events for our members, create meeting schedules and websites, gather resources, and balance the books. We communicate with other NA communities and the Fellowship as a whole. We participate in fellowship development. We get involved with literature creation or translation, and provide learning days and workshops so that members can participate in the life of Narcotics Anonymous. All of this and more goes to build our Fellowship. Keeping the connection in view between the service we do and the addict who walks in the door brings passion to our service, and keeps us focused on our purpose.

There are no menial tasks in Narcotics Anonymous. If a newcomer were to go to a meeting and find an empty room, it wouldn't matter how many committees we had; the addict would not get the message. We need members who set up the meeting and make the coffee as much as we need the member who chairs or speaks. Keeping our primary purpose in mind helps us to remember what is important, and to serve in a way that moves us toward our goals. Stewardship is care of something entrusted to us. Each of us as a member has responsibility for our group and our Fellowship. We may practice that actively in service, or simply by participating in meetings in a spirit of respect and care.

Each of us matters in Narcotics Anonymous. We may not like each other or understand the purpose a troublesome member serves, but every one of us is as important as every other. For some of us, the experience of being heard and respected is entirely new. We may treasure that as a gift, or we may constantly test it. It can take a lifetime to believe that we are valued.

Our trusted servants are also addicts who sometimes suffer, and treating them like bad employees won't get the message carried to them or through them. A trusted servant in one area was doing a terrible job, coming to every service meeting angry and leaving discord and frustration in his wake. An experienced member shook her head and sighed, "He acts like nobody loves him." Being able to address a member as a suffering addict rather than as a problem—or as just the service position they hold—allows the dynamic to change from bitterness to empathy. Even when we have to take action to remove a trusted servant or recover lost assets, we can be mindful of our reaction. Allowing someone their dignity when they're doing wrong gives them the space to recover even as we hold them accountable. We carry a message in the way we address challenges and problems. Tradition Five reminds us that our first job is to make sure our trusted servants can keep coming back, no matter what.

At its heart, Tradition Five is about communication. Carrying the message is a matter of communicating with the suffering addict in a language he or she can hear and understand. For some of us, that's the language of the heart. Others of us respond better to information, and still others aren't persuaded by words at all: We need to see in order to come to believe. Concept Eight tells us that "our service structure depends on the integrity and effectiveness of our communications," and it serves us well to remember that part of what we do in learning to carry a conscience, or to relay information back and forth between different service bodies, is also practice for carrying the message.

Being responsible in service is one of the ways we learn to be responsible in our lives, and of course accountability is critical in our trusted servants. Our experience in service allows us to feel ownership of our Fellowship. It's ours. Our lives depend on Narcotics Anonymous, and NA only exists through our shared efforts. Serving together builds mutual respect and deep love for our program. Whether or not we see service at the center of our recovery, everything we do to participate in NA serves to further our primary purpose, to strengthen and build Narcotics Anonymous for ourselves and the addict yet to come.

WORKSHOP QUESTIONS

The questions below offer a way to begin—or continue—a service discussion or workshop focused on this Tradition.

1. What are some of the differences in how groups and service bodies practice Tradition Five?

2. How does the work of this body support NA's primary purpose? Do we have other purposes as well?

3. How do we support groups in carrying an inclusive message? How do we support groups in addressing challenges?

4. How does remembering our primary purpose focus our service priorities? How do the roles and efforts of our boards and service committees relate to the primary purpose? How do we bring our primary purpose into all of our service efforts?

5. How well are we carrying the message of recovery? What limits are there in our efforts to carry the message? How much do we rely on facilities in our community to get addicts into our meetings?

6. How can we consider the needs of those members or potential members who are missing from our meetings? Can we strive to meet the needs of more addicts while staying focused on our primary purpose? What can we do to reach addicts who are physically unable to attend meetings?

7. What does our public image have to do with our primary purpose? Why is it important to carry a consistent message from one community to the next, from one country to the next, and around the world?

8. How does this Tradition help us understand anonymity? How does anonymity help us understand this Tradition? How do we practice anonymity in terms of this Tradition?

9. Discuss any bridges between this Tradition and one or more of the Twelve Concepts. What do these bridges teach us about our service efforts?

10. What more can we do to bring the principles of this Tradition into our service efforts? What could we do differently to better carry out our services?

A Vision for NA Service begins with the declaration that "all of the efforts of Narcotics Anonymous are inspired by the primary purpose of our groups. Upon this common ground we stand committed." The common ground of our primary purpose allows us to set aside differences and work together. With a clear view of our purpose, we can set priorities. Everything we do in Narcotics Anonymous is ultimately in service to that purpose: carrying the message to the addict who still suffers.

When our groups are focused on their primary purpose of carrying the message, things have a way of simplifying naturally. When we allow ourselves to believe that an addict, any addict, can stop using drugs, lose the desire to use, and find a new way to live, it brings great hope into our lives. We begin to see the possibility of recovery for the addict suffering and for ourselves. We come to understand that if a transformation so deep is possible in the earliest stages of our recovery, the possibilities for us to change as we continue to practice these principles are truly without limit. The message of hope isn't just for the addict walking in the door. Our recovery, like our disease, is progressive. Each of us is a miracle. No matter how far we have come, opportunities for spiritual growth and freedom from addiction are still available to us. Our message is hope and the promise of freedom, and it's true for us every day we choose to recover.

An NA group ought never endorse, finance, or lend the NA name to any related facility or outside enterprise, lest problems of money, property, or prestige divert us from our primary purpose.

TRADITION

6

In Step Six, the Basic Text reminds us, "Being human we will wander off course." We don't always notice when we're wandering: This is the great challenge for many of us in practicing meditation, or even sitting in a meeting. Just staying in our seat without checking our phone or creating side conversation can be surprisingly difficult, especially when we are having feelings we'd rather avoid. Tradition Six suggests that the things that divert us are mostly those we use to feed self-obsession. When we let go of the illusion that things outside ourselves will fill that empty place inside, we can stop distorting tools into weapons we turn on ourselves.

The better we get at staying present with the things that truly matter to us, the more able we are to understand our Higher Power's will for us and find the power to carry that out. One way to start is to recognize that the newcomer really matters to us, and that it's up to us to ensure that the message comes through.

When we resist the impulse to get diverted,
to wander off course, we are present for the miracle.
The life we save might be our own.

Tradition Six

Tradition Six teaches us to be true to ourselves. The Sixth Tradition explains why the NA message must be clear. If we are to keep from being diverted, we must know what our purpose is. We can't just sort of know; we must be certain. We have a message, and our purpose is to carry it. Anything else is a distraction or a diversion. Distraction steals our attention; diversion, our energy, and both take us away from what matters to us. Addiction painfully diverted us from our hopes and dreams. Tradition Six suggests that the things most likely to divert us now—as groups and as individuals—seem like they could benefit us, but will betray us in the long run. Even if we are not vigilant about our message, our autonomy, and our principles from the beginning, we will soon find that we must practice the Twelve Traditions in order to survive.

Practicing Tradition Six has much in common with the practice of Step Ten. When we keep an eye on our actions and relationships through the practice of regular inventory, we can recognize our tendency to wander off course before we have gone very far. Each of the motives this Tradition mentions that leads us off course—money, property, and prestige—is not a problem until it becomes a problem. But desire for these things can spin out of control when we experience a character defect like insecurity.

Tradition Six breaks naturally into three parts: the things we should not do, why we should not do those things, and what will happen if we do. Each of the actions we are warned about is a compromise; each of the reasons is a roadblock; ultimately, the result is that we lose sight of our purpose. We are diverted.

We don't often get diverted by things that are obviously unrelated to NA and our primary purpose. However, when it comes to issues that seem closely aligned with our primary purpose, the lines are not so clear. Treatment clinics, organizations, bureaus, churches, and other programs all try to help addicts recover. NA is not those other organizations, nor are we the same as any other fellowship. We don't use literature or speakers from outside of NA. Over and over, we check ourselves not only for affiliation, but for the appearance of it.

Much of what we do in NA puts us in contact with the world outside our Fellowship. We rent space for our meetings; we carry our message into institutions; often we are obliged to help big institutions, including governments, to understand what Narcotics Anonymous is, and that addicts do recover. In many places it has been illegal for addicts to meet at all. From our early history to our present-day service in new NA communities, making it possible for addicts to recover means demonstrating that addicts do recover. We are our best evidence. We are examples of our program and examples of our faith in NA when we act on that faith and stand on our principles "with neither aggressiveness nor fear."

Staying focused on our primary purpose can be very difficult. We know how important it is to carry the message, and it's easy to feel inadequate. In order to practice Tradition Six we must believe that we have what we need to carry out our purpose. Sometimes that requires creativity, and sometimes it requires patience. When we really get a sense of the power of the NA message and the importance of the action we take in our Twelfth Step, the work takes on a kind of urgency that can drive us to cut corners, compromise, or allow ourselves to be taken in by promises. We have too much on the line to gamble with the NA name. A simple, clear message, delivered honestly and without any confusion or controversy, saves lives.

 ## WORD BY WORD

Define, expand on, or clarify the words or phrases from this Tradition, one at a time or in relation to each other, for writing or discussion with your sponsor or other NA members.

Example: prestige

Although the word *prestige* commonly refers to admiration or respect, its origins refer to illusions or trickery. At its root, then, prestige is often false: an illusion. In a Fellowship where we are all equal, where anonymity is our spiritual foundation, the illusion of prestige is particularly destructive. Whether we believe our job is impressive, or our service is visible, or we think our cleantime gives us rank or clout among our peers, seeking prestige in Narcotics Anonymous means we are setting ourselves apart. Doing so is not only toxic to the atmosphere of recovery, it is incredibly dangerous for us personally. We dismiss most of the people who could save our lives as not good enough. A member shared, "My ego has taught me more about the Twelve Traditions than anything else." We are liable to seek false prestige when we don't believe we can be loved for who we are. When we learn the painful lesson that prestige tends to be hollow, false, illusory—not at all the respect, dignity, and value we were seeking—we are able to experience real connection with ourselves, our fellows, and our Higher Power.

 ## SPIRITUAL PRINCIPLES

Each Tradition embodies a variety of spiritual principles. The list of principles and values below may be useful as we consider applications of this Tradition. Explore them in writing or discussion with your sponsor or other NA members. If other principles or values not listed below seem relevant for you, include those as well.

• integrity	• faith	• harmony	• anonymity
• humility	• awareness	• dignity	• fidelity
• vigilance	• balance	• respect	• loyalty
• confidence	• prudence	• conviction	• perseverance

Example: vigilance

Often we think of vigilance in almost military terms, as if we were standing watch against incoming hostilities. In addition to caution and watchfulness, vigilance means sustained concentration or attention, as when people hold a vigil. Prayer and meditation are both practices of sustaining attention. When we understand vigilance as a peaceful principle, rather than a warlike one, we can practice it in a spirit of unity, goodwill, and faith.

We remain vigilant about our own actions and also about the actions of those around us, but ensuring the integrity of our program does not require us to be unkind. Rather, we watch our own motives, careful to avoid situations that would risk the endorsement, financing, or lending of the NA name mentioned in Tradition Six. We are happy to work cooperatively, but vigilance means that we take care to ensure that others don't mistake our willingness to be cooperative for endorsement or affiliation. When we firmly, politely, and clearly explain ourselves and our limits, we make it easy to understand and respect those boundaries.

For Members

Although this Tradition addresses itself to the groups, the issues it warns us about arise on a personal level, too: Money, property, and prestige can divert us because each of them can be used to feed self-centeredness. This Tradition points us to the very personal investments each of us has in our groups and in our Fellowship. Our personal practice of humility and anonymity serves the group as much as ourselves.

One of the hallmarks of our disease is that it takes us away from the things that matter to us. We may have dreams or goals, people we love and care about, spiritual values, religious faith—but none of it matters when we are using. Addiction diverts us, over and over, until we feel completely hollowed out. It's that empty feeling in our gut that we'd do just about anything, even die, rather than feel. Sometimes that feeling follows or revisits us deep into our recovery.

Practicing Tradition Six as a member means recognizing the ways our personal affiliations can affect the group, and also how desire for money, property, or prestige can impact our personal practice of unity. When we consider this Tradition in our own lives, we often begin by noticing how we respond to what attracts us. Many of us appreciate having nice things. We value being respected in our community. Being regarded well by others may be important enough for us to pay attention to our behavior and our self-presentation—or it may be so important that we base our own sense of ourselves on how we think others are seeing us.

When we feel like we're not enough, we become vulnerable in ways we may not recognize. We may be unsure of ourselves or unsure of our Fellowship, our message, or our principles. Particularly when we're stepping out into a new area, standing firm on these issues can seem like a luxury. We think we'll do that later, when we're more established. Or perhaps we suspect some of the principles of our Traditions are more appropriate for NA communities with greater resources. In fact, nothing is further from the truth. We can't build a strong structure on a weak foundation, in our lives or in our Fellowship.

In the rooms of NA, there are doctors and lawyers, counselors and health care workers, and others whose professional lives intersect our primary purpose in some way. Tradition Eight offers more guidance about the relationship between our occupations and NA membership, but Tradition Six reminds us to watch for the appearance of endorsement or affiliation in meetings. For example, we consider whether wearing uniforms or insignia in a meeting could imply affiliation, set us apart, or send the wrong impression to those attending meetings with us.

To endorse is to openly support an organization or a person. Each of us may have causes or candidates or belief systems, schools or churches or even treatment centers that we personally support. But keeping those things out of meetings protects us from conflicts that might distract us from our recovery. We don't need to leave our personalities at the door to participate in unity, but we do consider how and what we share in and around meetings, and whether that contributes to the primary purpose.

There is an enormous difference between lending our own name as individuals and lending the name of Narcotics Anonymous. If we are participating in public forums or social media, we consider how our various interests and affiliations are presented to the public. It's useful to remember that others may not be able to distinguish one member's personal beliefs from the principles of NA as a whole. Practicing awareness goes a long way toward protecting our integrity. We may not notice that our behavior carries a message, but in fact our actions speak loud and clear. "I had an NA sticker on my car," a member recalled, "and I was driving like Captain Road Rage. I made a gesture at another car, and later I saw that car at the meeting. I wanted to hide under my chair." When we wear or carry the NA name, we endorse NA—and we also suggest that NA endorses us. There is no way for someone unfamiliar with our program to understand the protection our principle of anonymity offers both members and the Fellowship as a whole.

Having the financial resources to meet our goals is a priority for some of us. Active addiction doesn't lend itself to financial security, and we may have a long way to go just to be able to meet our basic needs. There's nothing in our principles that speaks against wanting better for ourselves. In fact, practicing principles in all our affairs improves many areas of our lives. Being able to recognize and serve a purpose, to balance unity and autonomy, to recognize our values and know how to put them into practice—all these gifts of the Traditions help us to serve well in any role. But when our disease gets hold of our financial lives, we can be trapped in the feeling that there is never enough, no matter how much or how little we have. This fear can lead us back into obsession and compulsion, even as we rationalize that we are seeking "success."

We watch for that feeling of being diverted. We try to notice when the ways we are spending time and attention are not what's most important to us, or when we feel empty again. Tradition Six warns of diversions created by greed and pride, but the shadow side of those are fear and shame. Attention to the Sixth Tradition in our personal lives also points to an application of the Eleventh Step: It's by paying attention to what matters to us that we find a sense of purpose, direction, and meaning. When we live with integrity and purpose, our ability to recognize joy and fulfillment in our lives improves remarkably.

QUESTIONS FOR MEMBERS

The questions below offer a way to begin—or continue—the process of writing, reflection, and discussion of this Tradition with your sponsor or other NA members.

IN NA

1. What is my part in practicing the Sixth Tradition? What's my responsibility as a group member to help keep the group from being diverted?

2. How do my sharing and my actions help to clarify the distinction between NA and other organizations, facilities, and so on?

3. How does my understanding of Tradition Six influence how I share? How do I share truthfully about my experience in a way that doesn't seem to imply endorsement?

4. What types of "prestige" have I encountered or experienced as an NA member? How can prestige divert me from the NA message? How do I share about the blessings of recovery while keeping the focus on our message?

5. Do I get distracted or diverted by my judgments of others? How does my desire to judge or enforce this Tradition challenge unity or our message? How does listening for our message allow me to set aside distracting details?

6. Have I allowed myself to become diverted by money, property, or prestige in my personal affairs or in the course of my NA service? If so, what were the results?

7. Do I use my job, personal accomplishments, or service commitments to try to have more credibility or authority in NA meetings or in service?

8. Do I use my professional skills to serve NA or to set me apart? How can I maintain clarity in terms of how my professional relationships affect my NA membership? How do I keep my involvements in outside organizations separate from involvement in NA?

9. What examples have I seen of this Tradition helping us to carry the message? What freedom does our integrity afford me?

10. How does this Tradition help me understand anonymity? How does anonymity help me understand this Tradition? How do I practice anonymity in terms of this Tradition?

11. Describe any bridges between this Tradition and one or more of the Twelve Steps. What do these bridges teach me about my recovery?

12. What more can I do to put the principles of this Tradition into action? How would applying this Tradition change my attitudes and actions?

IN ALL OUR AFFAIRS

13. How have I applied this Tradition outside NA? How else might the principles of this Tradition guide my thinking or my actions?

14. How does the Sixth Tradition help bring clarity to my decision making? What really matters to me? How do I stay focused on that? How do I align my priorities according to my own sense of purpose?

15. When am I most likely to compromise my values in trying to reach a goal? What are some ways I justify or rationalize those compromises? What are the consequences?

16. Where else do I find spiritual help or support? How do I reconcile my membership in NA with the other affiliations I might have? Can I keep my message clear from one place to another without being phony, or holding part of myself back?

17. What do I notice about my thoughts, feelings, or actions when I am getting confused or diverted?

18. What freedom does integrity afford me?

For Groups

Traditions Five and Six are so closely related that it is difficult to talk about one without the other. Our purpose is to carry the message to the addict who still suffers. We can only do that when we know what our message is—and what it is not. Tradition Six supports our primary purpose by reminding us to stay focused. If we allow ourselves to give our endorsement, our name, or our resources, we lose the power of our message. When we keep sight of the fact that our message makes us who we are, we have no need for affiliation or endorsement.

The NA message thrives when our groups are autonomous. One of the ways we remain attractive is by remaining unaffiliated. When a group is serving its primary purpose in a spirit of unity and openness, meetings naturally feel hopeful and safe.

Endorsement is lending approval to something. It may be direct, like an advertisement or an announcement of another organization's event, or indirect, as when a number of members all share about the same outside organization or experience. People come to understand the NA program in our meetings, and it's in meetings that we can get most confused. Vigilance from the start serves us well in Tradition Six. By remaining vigilant about our message, our autonomy, and our principles from the beginning, NA in our community can rely on the Twelve Traditions as a source of guidance as we build, rather than as an emergency net when things come crashing down. We check ourselves not only for endorsement and affiliation but also for the appearance of either.

We each carry the message in our own way, and we have a right to a spirituality of our own understanding. Other paths are part of many of our stories, but detailed sharing about what we do outside NA can quickly become something other than the NA message. We consider the effect our sharing may have, especially when many members in a group have something in common. When a number of members share about the same outside organization or the same religion, it can seem as if a group is endorsing that, or having that shared experience is necessary to be a member of that group or to recover in NA.

The ways in which we seem to endorse can be subtle. When we meet in a facility decorated with symbols or logos from other organizations, it can be hard to avoid the impression that we have affiliations. We may try to change the appearance of the room, or make clear through our format or readings that we are separate from the facility.

Facilities are not bound by our Twelve Traditions, but NA groups may request cooperation in order to uphold our principles. Just as we help our members understand how and why we carry a clear message without bullying or shaming people for how they share, we politely and clearly explain to those outside NA what our principles are and why they are important to us. Our ability to do this requires that we ourselves understand what our message is, what it means to protect it, and where those boundaries need to be.

Groups often need to ensure that it's clear we are not affiliated with the facilities where we meet. If group members happen to work in the facility, for example, the line between NA and the facility may become blurred. One group struggled when staff at their meeting place got in the habit of walking in and out of the meeting room throughout the meeting; it was very easy for newcomers to get the impression that the facility ran the meeting. Occasionally a meeting has had to move to protect itself, but most of the time, communication is the answer to these challenges. The *Public Relations Handbook* offers useful advice on relationships with facilities in which we meet.

Nonaddicts, including government officials, are welcome at open meetings. However, if they are coming regularly, we may want to have a polite conversation about the need for addicts to have a safe place to meet, free from outside influence or surveillance. A member from a place with a strong government presence was asked how they handled frequent "visits" from law enforcement. He smiled and said, "We try to see an opportunity for PR." Changing our perspective on limitations outside our control can help us find solutions.

One of the most important ways we protect ourselves from endorsement or affiliation is to be self-supporting. Traditions Six and Seven support each other in helping to keep our Fellowship alive and free. NA groups are rarely asked directly to finance an outside enterprise, but that may be the result when rent is inflated out of proportion, or when an organization asks us to contribute literature and supplies on an ongoing basis to support their work. The relationship can be just as far out of balance if a facility is subsidizing rent for a group or offering space for no charge. The group may need to better define its relationship with the facility. Sometimes, public relations committees or trusted servants may help sort out what is appropriate. Finding a balance where we are neither supporting nor being supported by another organization takes time and thought.

It's clear that a center is using our name inappropriately if they advertise that they provide NA services. When an NA meeting is listed in the bulletins, flyers, or signs for a facility, on the other hand, they may simply be making it easier for addicts to find us. Thoughtful group discussion on the issue can help us to arrive at a decision and determine how to communicate effectively and appropriately. We may simply ask the meeting facility that lists the NA meeting in their schedule to do so in a way that makes it clear we're not affiliated. Vigilance and diplomacy help us to protect the NA name while also maintaining the cooperative relationships that are so important to our survival.

Tradition Six protects us from diversions that might seem more about the individual than the group: pride, concern with perception by others, and insecurity. But groups can get caught in these issues just as easily. A group can easily shift from enthusiasm to arrogance. The group may start referring to itself as "the best" or begin competing with other groups for status or members. It can start small—groups competing over the quality of their refreshments, or throwing progressively bigger parties—and it soon gets out of hand. A group with an ego investment in its events may stumble into a host of problems. Events get expensive. Hoarding money begins to seem more important than participating in the fund flow to carry the message. Owning more supplies requires greater expense and effort to store and manage. When the group has been diverted from our primary purpose, we serve the things that once served us.

It's up to us as members of a group to notice when our group is being diverted. If we wait until diversions create a problem, we tend to experience our Traditions as things we argue about rather than as principles that help us carry the message and recover in unity. When we make small corrections before there is a big problem, our principles quietly guide us.

GROUP INVENTORY QUESTIONS _____

The questions below offer ways to begin—or continue—group inventory or discussion focused on this Tradition.

1. Why are issues of money, property, and prestige such a slippery slope for us? How have we seen them divert us from our primary purpose?

2. How can issues of affiliation and pursuit of money, property, and prestige affect the atmosphere of recovery in our group? What else can divert our group from our primary purpose? What can we do as a group to avoid these distractions? How can we regain focus, once diverted?

3. What is an endorsement? In what ways could our group be seen as giving an endorsement of something outside NA? How could or would doing so damage our reputation and our efforts to carry the NA message?

4. How do we maintain integrity as a group? How does the use of NA literature and speakers help us to practice that integrity?

5. How do autonomy, cooperation, and affiliation relate to one another? How do we exercise creative freedom in a way that honors the guidance of Tradition Six?

6. Why do we hold our meetings in this particular location? How do we keep our relationship with the facility one of cooperation, not affiliation? How do we help members understand our relationship with facilities where we meet? What is our relationship to clubhouses or meeting halls?

7. What can we do as a group to maintain or improve our relations with outside entities? How should we handle our disagreements with outside facilities or organizations?

8. How do we support members in learning the importance of our policy of nonaffiliation? Do the words and actions of our trusted servants honor this Tradition? How loving and caring are we in the way we help our members understand Tradition Six?

9. Do our efforts to keep our message clear sometimes make it seem like we're creating additional requirements for membership? How can our group practice this Tradition without limiting our inclusiveness?

10. How does this Tradition help us understand anonymity? How does anonymity help us understand this Tradition? How do we practice anonymity in terms of this Tradition?

11. Discuss any bridges between this Tradition and other Traditions. What do these bridges teach us about our group?

12. What more can we do to bring the principles of this Tradition into our group efforts? What could we do differently to better fulfill our primary purpose?

In Service

Tradition Six mentions groups in particular, but the boards and committees that serve and support the groups are often in a position to practice this Tradition as well. So much of the work we do in carrying the NA message through public relations, hospitals and institutions, phonelines, and the internet bring us into contact with other organizations. Finding the balance between cooperation and endorsement can be very challenging. Our service materials, including the *PR Basics* booklet, have guidance on both how we make these decisions and how to come to an understanding of our principles in practice. We turn to the guidance of our literature, our service materials, and our experienced members as we build these relationships.

We may believe that this guidance is only important in the beginning of a cooperative relationship, but as relationships develop over time we may be more likely to slide into endorsement or affiliation than we might have been in the beginning. These ongoing relationships are important to our ability to reach addicts. For our relationships with outside enterprises to remain strong, we must maintain the boundaries established by Tradition Six. Our name, our time, our people, and our money are all resources that we need to steward wisely. These resources add to our efforts to carry the message. If we allow them to be used for the purposes of another, we reduce our ability to reach addicts who may need us.

In one area, PR work with the department of corrections was so effective that NA became a standard part of corrections planning for drug offenders. A member of the committee who was also a treatment professional was hired to help implement new drug court programs. Although that member knew he was working as an individual and not as a member or representative of NA, it was hard for inmates and correctional officers to understand that—or believe it. Many newcomers got the impression that NA was part of their probation. When local government changed parties, that program ended— and with it, any involvement of NA with the corrections system. The new officials believed NA to be part of another political party, and out it went.

Challenges to our independence and identity tend to result from our best intentions more than our worst. The desire to destroy or compromise NA is something we see very rarely. Much more often, the NA name is compromised from either expediency or doubt that NA can stand on its own feet. We see the urgency, the desperation of addicts suffering, and standing on principle seems like it's getting in the way of helping addicts. Compromising our values—believing that the ends will justify the means—teaches us painfully that our message is only as strong as our belief in it. Staying true to our message and our principles ensures our integrity and that of our message.

A Vision for NA Service says that we aspire to a time when "every addict in the world has the chance to experience our message in his or her own language and culture and find the opportunity for a new way of life." To fear that addicts in some places cannot receive or carry our message—that their culture or circumstances are too challenging for NA to offer what we have been freely given—would be a lack of faith in the power and beautiful simplicity of the NA program. We neither force our message nor hold it back, but we do guard it as our most precious possession. Tradition Five reminds us that our message "is all we have to give." Humility is accepting ourselves exactly as we are. In a spirit of humility, we carry the NA message exactly as it stands, with no need for affiliation or endorsement, and allow NA to take root and grow naturally.

WORKSHOP QUESTIONS

The questions below offer a way to begin—or continue—a service discussion or workshop focused on this Tradition.

1. How does our policy of nonaffiliation protect our reputation, and how does that help us to carry the message? What is the difference between reputation and prestige?

2. What is the reputation of NA in this community? How do we serve that reputation, or compromise it? Have there been times when we've been tempted to justify or rationalize affiliation or endorsement if it seems to benefit NA in some way?

3. What responsibilities do we have for protecting the NA name? How do our decisions about local events, NA merchandise, and NA literature reflect this responsibility?

4. What other organizations do we come in contact with? What part can these contacts play in helping us to carry our message? What is the importance of building and maintaining effective relationships with outside organizations?

5. What can we do to ensure harmony with outside organizations? What is our responsibility in maintaining the integrity of that relationship?

6. Can we have a cooperative effort with other fellowships without compromising our message or feeling obligated to those other organizations? How can we cooperate without affiliation when we ask nonmembers to become involved in an NA event?

7. How do we engage in cooperative relationships with others in ways that do not constitute affiliation or endorsement? How do we practice Tradition Six in our relationships with merchandise vendors, venues for meetings or events, clubhouses or meeting halls, and so on?

8. Under what circumstances would it be acceptable for an outside organization or facility to print the NA name on materials, such as flyers or a website? When would it be inappropriate to do so? What should we do if a facility uses our name in an inappropriate manner?

9. When internal controversy diverts us from our primary purpose, how do we get back to unity? What principles help us continue to serve our primary purpose, even when we disagree with each other?

10. How else might our service committees be diverted from supporting the NA groups? How can we correct our course without losing unity or momentum?

11. How does this Tradition help us understand anonymity? How does anonymity help us understand this Tradition? How do we practice anonymity in terms of this Tradition?

12. Discuss any bridges between this Tradition and one or more of the Twelve Concepts. What do these bridges teach us about our service efforts?

13. What more can we do to bring the principles of this Tradition into our service efforts? What could we do differently to better carry out our services?

As members and as a Fellowship, we exist in the larger world. Membership in NA is not an exclusive contract. Many of us are involved in other organizations, seek help and spiritual guidance elsewhere, or find tools we appreciate in places other than NA. The importance of leaving those things at the door is not that they don't work or can't work, but simply that they are not NA. As members, we bring our experience, strength, and hope in recovery to the rooms of NA, allowing our other involvements and affiliations to remain anonymous. As groups and in service, our efforts to carry the message often bring us into contact with others outside of NA. Tradition Six guides us to take care that our relationships with those we encounter are always grounded in cooperation, not affiliation.

We seek to recover in an atmosphere of unity and anonymity, and we want to extend that opportunity to others as well. As groups and in service, we carry our message independent from the organizations and institutions we work alongside. Keeping our message clear ensures that each of us can recover—and that NA can do what it does best—without being diverted.

*Every NA group ought to be
fully self-supporting,
declining outside contributions.*

TRADITION

7

The practice of self-support is vital to our freedom. Over and over we describe addiction the same way: One is too many, and a thousand never enough. That feeling of "never enough" can stay with us long into recovery. It's hard to believe that our needs will be met, that we will be able to take care of the things that are important to us, or that we can ever feel content. Freedom from that desperation is part of a restoration to sanity. When we see that we can meet our own needs, we start to feel like we have a future.

Our self-supporting groups show us how to live. Each group meets its responsibilities and makes decisions in accordance with its resources and values. Money is part of that picture, but that's not our only resource. Self-support demands action and unity. Each of us contributes time, energy, creativity, experience, and love. When we commit to self-support, we take responsibility for our well-being and our future. We protect ourselves from outside influence.

The Seventh Tradition is our statement of abundance and sharing, fulfillment and support; our commitment to the addict who still suffers and to ourselves. Belief in self-support is a massive leap of faith. We commit to the idea that we will be enough. Even if our resources don't always keep up with our aspirations, we can stay clean and carry the message.

As long as we have each other and Narcotics Anonymous, we have all that we need. Our commitment to self-support doesn't mean we go it alone—it means we do it together.

Tradition Seven

From the first meetings we attend, many of us know this as "the money Tradition," setting the foundation for our financial practices. However, Tradition Seven is about much more than money. Tradition Seven is a key to our unity and independence. Self-support ensures that our message stays clear and true, that we remain uncompromised and unaffiliated. The commitment to self-support is a challenge, and we grow in the process of meeting it.

Self-support is closely linked to the idea of self-determination: We are free to make our own decisions and set our own course. Our freedom is too valuable to be measured in money. And yet, having enough money to cover our expenses is part of how we maintain our freedom. If anyone outside NA supported us, they would inevitably end up with influence or control.

This is our Fellowship. We support it, we are responsible for it and to it, and we determine what Narcotics Anonymous stands for. As a Fellowship, we pay our own way, write our own literature, carry our own message, and work our own program. No one else has control or influence over our message. It's not stubbornness or pride that keeps this commitment strong; it's the knowledge—born of hard experience—that compromise on this principle consistently ends in disaster. Our history is full of moments when we confronted this choice; every time, our survival has depended on our willingness to stand firm.

Our commitment to self-support sends a unique and compelling message to the outside world as well. The fact that we are self-supporting changes the nature of the conversation we have with the public. We are not seeking donations or grants; we are not asking for anything but the chance to care and share the NA way. We offer a message of hope with no strings either for the addict who suffers or for the institutions with which we cooperate. In this way, Tradition Seven is closely related to the guidance offered by Tradition Six: Self-support is one of the many ways we avoid affiliation.

Through self-support, we demonstrate our commitment to each other. The work that we are able to accomplish through our voluntary contributions is remarkable. We have grown from a few groups to a worldwide Fellowship. Narcotics Anonymous thrives in countries all around the world, and our literature is available in many languages, because addicts have been willing to give freely and serve selflessly. Addicts get clean, experience recovery, and find a new way to live in Narcotics Anonymous in big cities, small towns, and rural areas; in well-established NA communities and in fledgling groups. When we step back and look at Narcotics Anonymous as a whole, the view is breathtaking.

 WORD BY WORD

Define, expand on, or clarify the words or phrases from this Tradition, one at a time or in relation to each other, for writing or discussion with your sponsor or other NA members.

Example: contribution

The roots of *contribution* mean, literally, to bring together. Each of us brings something to NA, and together we do what we could not do alone. When we make a contribution, whether to a conversation or to a basket, we are participating in something—we are part of it. We may contribute to a conversation by sharing our experience, or contribute to a service effort by sharing our time and energy. Contrast this with *donation,* which comes from the word meaning *gift.* We make donations to things we appreciate that are outside of ourselves; we contribute to things that we are a part of. We may donate to charity, but NA is not a charity. We contribute our time, energy, creativity, thought—and, yes, our money—to ensure that our Fellowship continues, that every addict has the opportunity to recover in NA, and that we remain alive and free. Every act of service, no matter how small, is a contribution demonstrating our commitment and our gratitude.

SPIRITUAL PRINCIPLES

Each Tradition embodies a variety of spiritual principles. The list of principles and values below may be useful as we consider applications of this Tradition. Explore them in writing or discussion with your sponsor or other NA members. If other principles or values not listed below seem relevant for you, include those as well.

- gratitude
- anonymity
- dignity
- sacrifice

- responsibility
- freedom
- generosity
- unity

- faith
- prudence
- humility
- autonomy

- integrity
- simplicity
- commitment

Example: generosity

The practical direction offered by Tradition Seven—declining outside contributions and supporting ourselves—asks us to put the spiritual principle of generosity into action. We only keep what we have by giving it away, and learning how to give responsibly and effectively may be part of our Twelfth Step as much as our practice of Tradition Seven.

We hope that another addict will receive what was so freely given to us, and we express that hope by giving generously of ourselves to help NA fulfill its primary purpose. Practicing generosity takes discipline. It does not mean giving beyond our means, or making promises we cannot keep. When we are involved in service to our local NA community, we see the value of stable, reliable contributions; we also learn that money is a very small part of what we offer. Time is irreplaceable, and may be the most precious gift we can give. Our time, our experience, our creativity, our hope, our money in the basket, and our attention in the meeting are all expressions of generosity and parts of our contribution to NA.

For Members

Even for those of us who don't see much of a link between the Traditions and our personal lives, Tradition Seven seems to have particular significance. Practicing self-support is a big change for most of us. Addicts and responsibility are a difficult combination. We tend to struggle with greed, jealousy, responsibility, and possessiveness. Often, we believe we have "money issues" when we are actually struggling with control, suspicion, insecurity, and fear. Tradition Seven offers us a road to freedom from those shortcomings as we learn to be accountable for ourselves.

Addiction is a greedy disease. It takes everything from us, and in turn we take from the people around us. We can see a clear connection between Step Nine and Tradition Seven when we recognize that being self-supporting is a form of amends to society and to the people who care about us. Each time an NA group or committee declines an outside contribution, it demonstrates that it is taking responsibility for itself. Our experience as individual members is not that different: As we clean up our wreckage and take responsibility for ourselves, we demonstrate our recovery to those who may have had quite enough of our hollow apologies. Making amends, taking on the project of self-support, and learning to live within our means are part of the process of being restored to dignity. Together, Tradition Seven and Step Nine offer restitution, restoration, and resolution.

The practice of humility helps us be honest about our circumstances. We learn to live and give within the limits of our lives. Discipline is not a practice that comes naturally to most addicts, and the need to say "no" to ourselves can be quite a challenge. "I wanted to buy dinner for my sponsor," an addict shared. "She wouldn't let me because she knew I couldn't afford it. It was humbling, but it helped me realize I don't have to pretend to be where I'm not."

We all go through times when we need help of one kind or another. Asking for help may be as principled and as difficult as anything we ever do. Practicing Tradition Seven in our personal lives doesn't mean that we never need assistance, but that we are honest with ourselves about the help we need and its price—financially and spiritually. When we care for ourselves to the best of our ability, we grow in self-respect, and our relationships with others begin to change as well.

Living in accordance with Tradition Seven does not mean that we become fiercely independent or isolated in our autonomy. The principles of this Tradition guide us to take responsibility for ourselves and our decisions. We think about our choices and their consequences, and come to understand the relationship between the choices we make and the things that happen to us. In our reading "Why Are We Here," we say, "Through our inability to take personal responsibility, we were actually creating our own problems." Many years into recovery we may see this pattern repeat. The solution is described by the problem—taking personal responsibility frees us from our self-made prisons, and opens us to alternatives and choices we may never have imagined.

Being honest with ourselves about our financial reality is part of practicing this Tradition. We may ask ourselves what is appropriate for us to contribute to NA. Considering this question in the larger context of our lives helps us make a more responsible decision than when we dig in our pocket for change at any given meeting. One member shared, "When I was new, I panhandled so I'd have something to put in the basket. Another addict found out, and told me to come to the meeting early and help set up chairs instead. He said they needed *me* at the meeting more than the money." Our money in the basket is no more or less important than our attention to the speaker or our hand on the broom. It takes both money and time to do what we do, and contributing what we can when we can makes that possible.

As a member of an NA group, we take part in developing a conscience about how the group will meet its responsibilities and participate in the life of the larger Fellowship. We are called upon to think about the resources and values of the group and NA in our community in relationship to our primary purpose, and to consider our personal relationship to NA as a whole. As we get involved in our home group and start to understand more about Narcotics Anonymous, we turn our attention to the basket—sometimes with great suspicion. Curiosity about where our money goes and how it is spent drives many of us to learn about NA service and how it works. When trusted servants meet that suspicion with empathy and openness, it defuses our fear. We keep the focus on the primary purpose not only when we are making decisions about our resources, but also when we explain how NA works. Honest and open communication allows each of us to feel safe and included.

We are called to consider this Tradition at every meeting when the basket is passed. The reminder that we are fully self-supporting is also a commitment to the newcomer. We ensure that NA will remain nonaffiliated, and that a desire to stop using will always be the only requirement for membership. We commit to making sure NA will be here when an addict reaches out for help. We may express that commitment in many ways; ultimately, it is how our gratitude speaks.

QUESTIONS FOR MEMBERS _____

The questions below offer a way to begin—or continue—the process of writing, reflection, and discussion of this Tradition with your sponsor or other NA members.

IN NA

1. How do I contribute to the well-being of the groups I attend? How else do I contribute to NA? How has this changed since I first came to NA?

2. Do I do my part to help NA remain self-supporting? What is the relationship between my gratitude and my contributions? What are some additional ways I could express my gratitude?

3. How do I decide how much money to contribute to NA? Do I plan ahead, budget, or give the same amount every time? Do I contribute at every meeting? Do I give in other ways?

4. How do my contributions compare to what I gave in my first year? Do I give more or less than I did when I attended more meetings? Do I give as much as the newcomers around me?

5. How do I know when I'm giving too much or too little? What's the right level of contribution of time and money for me right now?

6. What expectations do I have about how the money I put in the basket is spent? How do I find out about or have a say in those decisions?

7. What do I do when I am concerned about financial practices in NA? Do I ever act as if the amount of my contributions affects the importance of what I have to say?

8. How does this Tradition help me understand anonymity? How does anonymity help me understand this Tradition? How do I practice anonymity in terms of this Tradition?

9. Describe some of the bridges between this Tradition and one or more of the Twelve Steps. What do these bridges teach me about my recovery?

10. What more can I do to put the principles of this Tradition into action? How would applying this Tradition change my attitudes and actions?

IN ALL OUR AFFAIRS

11. How have I applied this Tradition outside NA? How else might the principles of this Tradition guide my thinking or my actions?

12. What has being a member of a self-supporting group taught me about self-support in other areas of my life? What does Tradition Seven teach me about living in society?

13. What does it mean for me to be self-supporting? What are some aspects of self-support beyond money? What are some spiritual or emotional benefits of self-support?

14. What does it mean to be self-supporting in my relationships or in other areas of my life?

15. How do I balance self-support with the need to sometimes accept help from others? What is the difference between self-support and self-reliance?

16. How does my application of Tradition Seven affect the way I live today?

For Groups

Protecting the integrity of the group is vital to maintaining the well-being of NA as a whole. As *The Group Booklet* points out, NA groups are the foundation of the NA service structure. Tradition Seven offers two instructions to the group, one conditional and one definite. The first, each group *"ought to be* self-supporting," is conditional. Groups are not always completely self-supporting; but if a group is not, any help it gets comes from within NA. For example, sometimes an NA community helps a group get started or continue to serve a clear need. The rest of the Tradition, "declining outside contributions," is absolute. We can never afford the cost of *outside* help, even when we cannot see how to manage on our own. The humility this Tradition asks for will help us keep our primary purpose in view with every decision we make.

We may all agree on the principle of self-support and still have very different understandings of what that actually means for our group. Each group is autonomous, and group practices vary widely. Groups do not tell each other whether or not to have refreshments, celebrations, or medallions; each group has choices about how to participate in the fund flow and how involved to be in the life of NA beyond its own doors. Still, we want to make informed decisions about our participation, keeping our primary purpose in mind. The links between Traditions Five, Six, and Seven are powerful. Each group determines its own values and circumstances, as well as its relationship to NA as a whole. Each time we make a decision about how to use our resources, we can put our priorities in order by asking, "How does this further our primary purpose?"

Groups don't just hold meetings. Some groups celebrate their anniversaries, sponsor marathon meetings or speaker jams, or hold picnics or holiday parties. Some groups also further the NA message by providing literature, offering support to existing events hosted by local service bodies, and participating in the fund flow by contributing to other levels of service. Groups benefit from thoughtful discussion about how an event or celebration supports NA unity and our primary purpose. Keeping in mind that NA funds and the time and energy of our trusted servants are limited resources, groups are responsible to think carefully about how these resources are used. Our Eleventh Concept reminds us that "NA funds are to be used to further our primary purpose, and must be managed responsibly."

Our commitment to self-support is an act of faith. That faith sustains us even when we fall on hard times, or when something unfortunate happens. Money is stolen; we lose meeting space or prices go up; we count on an event as a fundraiser and it flops. Where Tradition Seven calls on us to find ways to support ourselves, Tradition Two reminds us we can take the long view. Hardship can bring us together in unity, and prosperity can separate us if we are not careful. When we are willing to learn from our experience, a setback may be a call to action, not a link in an unbreakable chain. When we remember that there is but one ultimate authority, we can let go of the need to control or blame and remember that service is always a spiritual exercise. We trust each other, our Higher Power, and the conscience of our group.

No matter what happens, we want every addict to feel safe in NA. We trust our trusted servants, and we honor that trust by providing them with the tools and safeguards they need to be successful, including mentoring and support, service manuals, and local guidelines. We protect our trusted servants when we prevent large sums of money from being the responsibility of any one person. Participating in the fund flow rather than hoarding or holding large sums in the group treasury allows us to participate in the life of the Fellowship. This practice also reduces the risk or temptation that can come with large sums on hand. The *Treasurer's Handbook* can help the group keep good records and avoid unnecessary confusion.

Paying for meeting space is one way we demonstrate self-support. When facilities will not accept money, we find other ways to give back. We may ask the facility what we can do to carry our weight: We may help with cleaning or maintenance, or donate literature. However we give back, it's important that we do so consistently, and with a grateful heart. Every interaction with a facility is public relations; we set the tone for how we are seen in our community. In one town, the first NA meetings were known for loudness and bad behavior. It soon became difficult for new groups to find anywhere to meet. Taking responsibility for our group's relationship with the community around it is both an expression of self-support for our own group and a reflection on NA as a whole.

When a group is able to meet its own needs, contribute to the services beyond its doors, and plan responsibly, it shows in the atmosphere of the meeting. Good financial practices generate goodwill, even when need is great. When our actions are honest, open, transparent, and simple, they are trustworthy. Our commitment to self-support ensures that our groups walk our talk, and stand or fall on the power of the NA message—honest, simple, and true.

GROUP INVENTORY QUESTIONS _____

Choose questions from the list below—or create/adapt your own—to focus on as part of a group discussion or group inventory.

1. What are some ways to practice self-support besides money? How else do members contribute to this group? What does our group contribute to our local services?

2. Has our group ever needed to decline contributions from nonmembers? How did or would we go about doing so in a polite and respectful manner?

3. How does this group make decisions about how to spend our money? What do we need to fulfill our primary purpose? How do we tell the difference between wants and needs? Are we spending responsibly?

4. Does our group make contributions to other levels of service in order to help carry the message? What responsibility do we have for supporting the growth of NA in our community and beyond?

5. Are there things our group spends money on that aren't directly related to our primary purpose? Do we make a distinction between funds collected to carry out our primary purpose and other group expenses?

6. Does our group keep financial records? Have we noticed changes in our financial life recently? Over time? What decisions or discussions does this information prompt for us?

7. Does our group live within its means? How does our group make do when resources are scarce? Is it okay to pass the basket a second time?

8. What planning and resources were needed to get this group started? Where should help come from when starting a new meeting?

9. Does this group need a reserve of funds? Why or why not? What would be a reasonable prudent reserve? What other financial safeguards can we put in place to protect both our resources and our trusted servants?

10. Do we think we are entitled to a greater say in service decisions if we contribute more time, energy, or money? Do we allow any members of our group to give more than their fair share? What is a *fair share?*

11. Does our group depend on the contributions or literature purchases of newcomers to meet its budget? How can group members help to ensure that the weight of self-support doesn't fall on the newest members?

12. How does this Tradition help us understand anonymity? How does anonymity help us understand this Tradition? How do we practice anonymity in terms of this Tradition?

13. Discuss any bridges between this Tradition and other Traditions. What do these bridges teach us about our group?

14. What more can we do to bring the principles of this Tradition into our group efforts? What could we do differently to better fulfill our primary purpose?

In Service

Service bodies, like our groups, decline contributions from outside NA. Our service bodies, however, are not autonomous, and do not support themselves. Members and groups provide the direction and support necessary for our services to continue, and our service bodies operate within the means provided. Most of the time, in most of the Fellowship, our services operate on tight budgets. Strong faith and hard work created our Fellowship, and the same spirit of selflessness, resourcefulness, and joy in service sustains us today.

When we are excited about carrying the NA message through service, we can see how much there is to be done. Our enthusiasm brings NA to life, but it can also run away with us. When we commit to more than we can handle, we start feeling that old desperation creeping in. It takes time to build services that we can sustain and that will sustain us. It's our responsibility to keep an eye on whether our efforts in service are building up or burning out. The investment of time and energy that is called for in building solid, reliable services pays off in solid, reliable NA communities.

Self-support means we support the services that support us by providing the necessary time, money, training, and compassion. Our informational pamphlets *Money Matters* and *Funding NA Services* each offer thoughts and guidance about adequately supporting our services. We give not just to take care of ourselves, but to make our message available to addicts near and far. The money we give is not just for our group or for NA locally; the funds passed on to other levels of service help NA as a global Fellowship to fulfill our Vision for NA Service.

When we ask our service bodies to do something, we need to give them the resources to carry out our instructions—which means we will support them with our time, money, and enthusiasm. In addition to making sure we provide adequate support, we need to think about sustainability each time we ask our service bodies to take on a new commitment: Will our community be willing to support this over time? We discuss whether the level of commitment required is realistic for us, as well as other obligations that already exist. Trust in the process and in our Higher Power helps us sort out what we want, what we need, and what we can afford.

Our message is free, but carrying it is not. Money is a necessity to keep many of our services operating, and the money that comes in through the basket is not always sufficient to cover those costs. Much of what we accomplish in service is funded by income from events, merchandise, literature sales, and so on. This has been the subject of debate and contention at times, but the fact remains: The portion of our income that comes directly from member contributions does not pay for all that we do in NA service. Our practice of this Tradition is not served by lecturing one another about our inadequate contributions. As a Fellowship, we are often more willing to participate in fundraisers than to contribute directly. The responsibility rests with each of us to determine what balance of fund flow we consider acceptable, and to work toward that balance by stepping up in whatever way seems right to us. However, we do want to make sure that our efforts do not lead us to actively solicit money from those who are not members. For example, we may sell refreshments at an NA event, but we don't have a bake sale at a shopping center.

If our events begin to take on a greater sense of importance than supporting our groups or reaching addicts in our community, we might want to look at our priorities. We want to ask ourselves whether money is diverting us, whether it's contributing to our unity or our division, and whether we are losing our sense of purpose. Goodwill and enthusiasm are attractive, and when we can see our contributions in action, we want to give.

When fundraising starts to seem like the most important thing we're doing, our priorities are out of proportion. It can be very easy for a service body that is funding itself, or that is financially dependent on events and conventions, to lose touch with its accountability to the groups. Our Concepts remind us that our service boards and committees are always answerable to the groups we serve, and our Second Tradition reminds us that a Higher Power is ultimately in charge. Every NA service body can benefit from periodically checking to see that its priorities are properly aligned with the primary purpose, and a simple way to do so is to look at where our human and financial resources are allocated. Events or activities may be easier to find trusted servants for than public relations or H&I panels. By practicing the faith that is necessary in order to be self-supporting, we do a much better job of allowing a loving Higher Power to care for us.

As we read this, addicts are finding hope and freedom in jails and institutions all over the world. Isolated addicts are connecting with other NA members online, through the mail, and at conventions and service workshops.

They are bringing NA home to places it didn't exist before. Somewhere in the world, right now, addicts are gathered in a meeting of Narcotics Anonymous. All of this happens through the energy, love, hard work, commitment, and generosity of addicts who have come together in desperation and found a new way to live.

WORKSHOP QUESTIONS

The questions below offer a way to begin—or continue—a service discussion or workshop focused on this Tradition.

1. What does self-support mean for service bodies? What are the limits of self-support for service boards and committees?

2. Do our committees have the people, training, money, or other support that they need to carry out their work? How do we support those who serve us?

3. To what extent does this service body rely on funds other than group contributions to pay for our services? Have we experienced challenges related to fundraising? What potential challenges might we guard against?

4. What are our practices regarding activities or events that bring in money? What policies, guidelines, or general "do's" and "don'ts" do we follow?

5. Are our service priorities reflected in how we use our resources? How does our service body set priorities? Who do we involve in those conversations?

6. Do we communicate with those we serve in ways that are understandable and open? Are our accounting and accountability practices simple and transparent?

7. How do we set and evaluate our prudent reserve? Have we ever made use of it? What purpose does it serve in this service body? What is the difference between prudence and hoarding?

8. Do we have ways to prevent and/or address theft, misappropriation, and financial mismanagement? How do we protect our members and our resources at the same time? Does stealing disqualify someone from membership?

9. How do we determine whether it's appropriate for us to accept nonprofit discounts, room-block rebates, bulk-order discounts, or other incentive programs?

10. How does this Tradition help us understand anonymity? How does anonymity help us understand this Tradition? How do we practice anonymity in terms of this Tradition?

11. Discuss any bridges between this Tradition and one or more of the Twelve Concepts. What do these bridges teach us about our service efforts?

12. What more can we do to bring the principles of this Tradition into our service efforts? What could we do differently to better carry out our services?

Our tradition of self-support keeps us alive and free. We can be creative in the ways that we gather resources and careful in how we use them. We must be very cautious in our relationships with those outside the Fellowship, continually checking our practices and motives to ensure that we are not accepting gifts or support that might compromise our integrity. Tradition Seven invites us to learn more about integrity and what it means to stick to principle without being rigid or ungrateful. When we practice Tradition Seven, we don't just turn away the donations of others; we demand of ourselves that we step up and meet our responsibilities.

We learn that we can care for ourselves and meet our needs. We can thrive and grow as a Fellowship even when resources are really thin. Generosity is an antidote to fear, and when we give freely, our hearts are filled. The value of this Tradition may be hard to see when we are deciding not to ask for help from those outside NA who would gladly offer support, but Tradition Seven in our Basic Text reminds us that "Everything has its price." Practicing self-support allows us richness beyond measure. When we support ourselves responsibly—as individuals, as groups, and as a Fellowship—we are rewarded in confidence, dignity, and freedom. We are responsible members of society today, and the reward for that is hope for the future.

Narcotics Anonymous should remain forever nonprofessional, but our service centers may employ special workers.

TRADITION

8

Narcotics Anonymous is a Fellowship of people for whom drugs had become a major problem. We are recovering addicts who meet regularly to stay clean. How often have we heard these words, or something like them? At every meeting we are reminded that we come together to share our experience, strength, and hope. We don't need anything more than that to help each other.

Addiction is a deadly disease. We don't always see our struggle clearly when we are in it, but when we are clean and watch another addict in the grips, it's heartbreaking. We want so badly for them to get clean, but we may not feel qualified to help. In Narcotics Anonymous, we believe that no one is better qualified to help an addict than another addict in recovery. We share with each other our experience in addiction and the steps we took—and continue to take—to experience freedom.

Each of us has something to offer. We don't need specialized training to carry the message; all we need to do is pay attention. We give what was so freely given to us. When we share what is in our heart, even when we are in great pain, we connect. The simple, priceless gift we give each other is the recognition of our humanity.

We can't buy our way out of addiction, and we can't sell it either. Recovery is a gift, given freely, passed from hand to hand and heart to heart. Sharing our recovery restores our faith and gratitude. Seeing that we are not alone frees us from the isolation and alienation of addiction.

Narcotics Anonymous remains forever nonprofessional because what we give is beyond words, beyond measure. The very best we can give is ourselves— we give freely, and what we give is hope.

Tradition Eight

At a casual glance, Tradition Eight might not seem like one of our more "spiritual" Traditions, but in fact it reaches to the core of our spiritual program. By committing to being nonprofessional, we ensure that our simple way will be an enduring legacy—freely given among equals, our program is safe from the whims and fancies of the public. We are also free from any implied authority or expertise of our members. When we "come to an understanding of the program for ourselves," we become skilled at sharing our own recovery. No one certifies us as NA members, and no one can fire us. Our membership, our recovery, and our experience are ours alone.

Many of our members are professionals in their own right, including some who work with addicts, but we do not hire people to carry our message. Reaching out from addict to addict is an application of anonymity: We leave our professional identities at the door. In meetings, we are present to one another as equals, as addicts seeking recovery and carrying a message of hope, regardless of our titles or our relationships outside. Our trusted servants are not counselors or supervisors; our meetings are not classes or therapy groups. We come together to share our experience, and in Narcotics Anonymous we are all experts on our own stories. We may bring skills or experience with us, but we don't bring status. Our relationship to recovery and to service is simple; in NA, we are addicts who have found a way out, and that is what we share.

Nonprofessional is not the same as unprofessional. The term *nonprofessional,* for us, is a reminder that we freely carry the message to one another in an atmosphere of equality. The term *unprofessional,* on the other hand, means "below standard"—and that most certainly does not describe our service efforts. There is no room for professionalism in how we share the message with one another, but the same is not always true for how we carry out our services. We are reliable and responsible; we plan and execute our efforts in service to our goal of carrying the message; we keep records, honor contracts, pay fairly, and act according to the rules of the venues in which we meet. We understand that part of carrying an attractive message is ensuring that our behavior is appropriate. When we engage in public relations, our appearance is appropriate to our audience.

Tradition Eight's insistence that we remain a nonprofessional Fellowship allows each of us to recover and share as equals. No matter what direction life takes us in, we can continue to live and recover together in NA. Anonymity means that no matter who we are outside, how long we have been clean, or what we have done in NA service, we're just another member staying clean another day. Each of us has a message to carry, and we all need each other. Our beliefs about who or what we are, or how we think we are perceived, matter very little.

In some cases it's difficult or impossible to accomplish service tasks solely with members serving on a voluntary basis. Phoneline service is a common example: We want to ensure that addicts seeking help have a chance to talk to NA members, but many communities contract with an outside company to ensure that calls are always answered and properly forwarded. Our internet presence, as well, may need development or maintenance beyond our local abilities. We contract for those services we need to ensure that addicts seeking help can reach us.

We begin with a vision, and that vision becomes a reality. In the transition, maintaining spiritual obligations while meeting legal and administrative commitments may be deeply challenging. There are times when we need expert assistance, and situations where we need consistency, continuity, and accountability that would be impractical or unrealistic to ask of members on a voluntary basis. Tradition Seven reminds us that we cannot allow any member to give more than their fair share, but it may take thought and prayer to determine what that is. Asking members to bring an aspect of their professional identities into NA service can complicate the relationship between that member and NA, not just in obvious ways but also in ways we may not expect. As we look at that balance, we may realize that we need to hire someone—whether for a short time, as when we engage a lawyer to help us with legal issues, or over the long term, as when we employ someone to staff a local service office. The job of carrying our message is forever nonprofessional. Our trusted servants, special workers, and those we hire for specific tasks all perform duties that ultimately support our vision, serve our primary purpose, and help NA grow.

WORD BY WORD

Define, expand on, or clarify the words or phrases from this Tradition, one at a time or in relation to each other, for writing or discussion with your sponsor or other NA members.

Example: forever

It's unusual for a "just for today" program to use the word *forever.* Forever means without interruption, going forward into the future without end. It means we do something continually.

To say that we remain "forever nonprofessional" is a commitment. We are not *mostly* nonprofessional, or nonprofessional *as it serves us.* No matter what, in all cases, Narcotics Anonymous works the same way: one addict freely helping another. Our message is hope and the promise of freedom from active addiction. We believe that any addict can stop using drugs, lose the desire to use, and find a new way to live. As members of a nonprofessional program, we are the ones who carry our message, reach out to the suffering addict, and take care of our meetings and our services. We can see a clear relationship between this Tradition and Tradition Seven. Carrying our message freely, in a spirit of anonymity and equality, frees us from the obligations and controversies so common outside our doors.

SPIRITUAL PRINCIPLES

Each Tradition embodies a variety of spiritual principles. The list of principles and values below may be useful as we consider applications of this Tradition. Explore them in writing or discussion with your sponsor or other NA members. If other principles or values not listed below seem relevant for you, include those as well.

• humility	• prudence	• anonymity	• integrity
• surrender	• flexibility	• autonomy	• self-acceptance
• stability	• consistency	• accountability	

Example: humility

Humility is an honest assessment of the truth about ourselves, including our abilities and limitations. It can be hard for us to let go of the idea that we should be able to handle all of the challenges we face on our own. The fact that we can't do it ourselves all the time, that we sometimes need a little help from outside, may be humbling. We struggle with this surrender when we are new in NA, and whenever we return to the first few Steps. In service, we can become overloaded, burned out, and angry at other members who aren't doing what we think they should be doing. It is an act of humility and self-acceptance to admit when it makes sense to pay someone to carry out certain tasks for us.

We do what we can, and then step back. We don't hire professionals to facilitate or chair our recovery meetings or to do our Twelfth Step work for us, but there are some tasks that are either so specialized or so time-intensive that hiring someone makes sense. Balancing willingness and humility means that we are able to step up to the work we are able to do, and also admit that sometimes we need help.

For Members

Opportunities to practice Tradition Eight in our personal recovery aren't obvious to many of us at first. NA remains forever nonprofessional, but many of our members are professionals in their own right; practicing this Tradition does not mean that we turn away from our careers or pretend not to be who we are. Still, no matter what professional skills or knowledge we have— including about addiction, recovery, or spirituality—it's our direct personal experience that is valuable in Narcotics Anonymous. We freely share NA recovery with each other. Being ourselves and sharing our experience gives hope to the still-suffering addict. All of our service efforts come back to our primary purpose, creating opportunities for addicts to freely help one another. Each of us shares our experience, strength, and hope in our own way.

Tradition Eight builds on the guidance of Tradition Seven. Although we support ourselves through our own contributions, there are times when we need assistance. Asking for help is an act of humility, whatever the circumstance. There are many things we can do ourselves, but we all need help from time to time. Gaining clarity about our needs and capabilities frees us from dependency on one end of the spectrum and the illusion of self-sufficiency on the other. We work best when we remember to act in a spirit of humility, unity, and anonymity. Leadership skills in NA include holding our tongue, knowing our limits, and asking for help when we need to.

Service offers growth. We come into NA broken, and we learn how to live. Much of that learning happens in service; in fact, we expect one another to learn, grow, and develop new skills in service. Sponsorship, mentorship, learning days, and guidelines all help us learn to do the tasks set before us as we further our message. We know that this is an ongoing process, and demanding perfection can keep us from moving ahead at all. Our knowledge grows as we visit various types of service meetings. We learn to listen and find new interests. We may move from one kind of service to another; after a long time in public relations service, for example, we might focus our energy on group-level service for a while, or join an activities committee. It can be good for us and good for the local NA community when we try new roles, or when a new member dives into service.

We are nonprofessional, but we have high expectations for our trusted servants. Rising to meet those expectations is part of how we learn in service. The term *service* suggests that we are providing a service to NA, but the work we do for NA also serves us, allowing us to learn and grow with the experience. Many of us learn to keep financial records as a part of taking on a treasurer's commitment, or learn to facilitate a business meeting by chairing a service body. As trusted servants, we meet the challenges before us best when we are given the room to shine. When we try to control people or outcomes, we are diverted from our purpose. Nonprofessional does not mean that we are noncommittal, but it does mean that service is not a career for us. Ensuring that we remain a volunteer enterprise keeps us focused on our purpose rather than our personal ambition. Our recovery depends on Narcotics Anonymous.

Sponsorship is a nonprofessional relationship, passing on what was given to us. It may be intimate or rigid; for most of us, it's somewhere in between. But sponsors are not therapists, counselors, or parole officers. If we forget that sponsorship is not a professional relationship, we risk acting as if sponsors have authority, rather than experience to share. Or, we may risk treating our sponsor as an employee, to be "fired" or reprimanded when they don't meet our expectations.

Our professional identity and our life in NA may have nothing at all to do with each other. Or we may be very good at recognizing and maintaining boundaries between one and the other. But sometimes it is not so clear. For example, when a member who is a lawyer is asked to weigh in on a legal issue, or a member who is a chef is asked to cook for an event, both the member and the committee benefit from considering what boundaries are necessary and appropriate.

For members in some professions, there might be formal or informal restrictions that seem to conflict with our recovery. A member shared, "I was working nights in a detox, and I really connected with this patient. I wanted to reach out to her when she was released, but the facility stipulated no contact between clients and employees for two years after release. It was hard to make peace between my job and my Twelfth Step. I was able to help her reach out to some women in the rooms who could help her." Another member explained, "Living and working in a small town, it was hard to go to meetings that were full of my clients. I drove to another town for meetings, even though it was far, so I could share freely."

When we do have specialized skills or knowledge, we may be asked by other members for advice, or we may do business with people we meet in the rooms. Some of us may be comfortable with this; for others, being addressed on the basis of our profession feels uncomfortable or unsafe. When business relationships sour, it can be hard to keep coming back to the same meetings or to allow others space to recover, without trying to build a case or defend ourselves. We all deserve the right to recover in dignity, and keeping our work separate from our lives in NA may be an important part of preserving that right for ourselves.

Many of us have training or specialization in a particular field; some of us are degreed and certified, and some of us work in addiction treatment in one way or another. We may be very proud of these accomplishments, and it can be difficult to separate recovery from our professional lives or education. Still, we are asked to leave our credentials at the door. In Narcotics Anonymous, we are all addicts seeking recovery. Tradition Eight does not mean we can never speak of what we do outside of NA. We do, however, have a responsibility to think about what we share and the message we carry. Navigating our professional identity in an anonymous Fellowship can be challenging. As members, we are here to share in the NA message, not to diagnose, advise, or consult.

QUESTIONS FOR MEMBERS

The questions below offer a way to begin—or continue—the process of writing, reflection, and discussion of this Tradition with your sponsor or other NA members.

IN NA

1. What is the difference between a professional and nonprofessional approach to recovery? How does our commitment to remaining nonprofessional protect the therapeutic value we find in NA?

2. How did I first experience the nonprofessional nature of Narcotics Anonymous? How do I practice it?

3. Do I have personal interaction with special workers? What has that taught me about NA?

4. Do I treat my service work as a career? Do I ever act as if my service in NA affects my value as a member?

5. What are the healthy boundaries between my work life and my membership in NA? How do I keep the focus on recovery rather than my job?

6. Does my work or other expertise come into the rooms in some way? Do I try to gain authority, power, or position in NA based on my profession or other expertise?

7. How does this Tradition help me understand anonymity? How does anonymity help me understand this Tradition? How do I practice anonymity in terms of this Tradition?

8. Describe any bridges between this Tradition and one or more of the Twelve Steps. What do these bridges teach me about my recovery?

9. What more can I do to put the principles of this Tradition into action? How would applying this Tradition change my attitudes and actions?

IN ALL OUR AFFAIRS

10. How have I applied this Tradition outside NA? How else might the principles of this Tradition guide my thinking or my actions?

11. Are there other areas in my life where my work life needs to be separated from my other interests? How do I practice that?

12. When do I need to call on professionals to help me in my life or work? How do I make the decision to hire someone to perform a task or solve a problem?

13. Do I try to do things myself that I really should turn over to a professional? Do I want other people to do things for me that I could or should do myself? What factors do I consider when making a decision?

14. Do I try to gain authority, power, or position in my professional life based on my membership in NA?

For Groups

Tradition Eight offers further understanding of how we create an atmosphere of recovery. The NA group is the first experience most of us have with the principle of anonymity in action, and our atmosphere of recovery depends on that anonymity. Our commitment ensures that we come to each other as equals, that we treat each other as peers, and that we don't mistake one or more members as authorities on NA recovery. Being nonprofessional is one of the keys to freedom in Narcotics Anonymous. Because we are not engaged with the work of professionals, we are free from the pressure to perform by the guidelines and standards they use, and we are free from the theories and clinical models that shape or determine their work with addicts. The NA message is a key to freedom, and we carry it just by telling the truth about our own lives.

Our groups don't hire professionals to moderate, facilitate, supervise, or lecture in our recovery meetings. We don't pay people to carry our message for us. The message is ours alone to carry; what we share freely with one another is priceless. There is no certification we could offer, no credential we could seek, that would make one addict better suited to reach another. Everything we do is summarized in the vision of the addict with two days telling the addict with one day that it works. The experience we share, the Steps we work, the late-night calls—all serve to remind us that one addict helping another is without parallel.

Part of creating an atmosphere of anonymity in our meetings involves creating meeting formats that help demonstrate our equality. Many groups structure their meetings in ways that discourage cross talk or other scenarios that could easily lead us to give advice rather than share our experience. Even when groups have a speaker or two share for the entire allotted meeting time, it's clear that these members are not authorities on NA, but simply members sharing their own recovery. Some groups experience situations in which one or two charismatic or influential members may begin to seem like authority figures, even without intending to do so themselves. "There was a couple who pretty much ran the meeting when I first started attending," one member shared. "The way everyone seemed to go to them for answers, it took me a while to realize they weren't the NA counselors." When groups find ways to encourage equal participation, we avoid giving newcomers the wrong impression.

Experienced group members aren't the only ones who may be mistaken for authority figures. When members who are professionals are allowed to leave those identities at the door, they have the chance both to freely share recovery—not expertise—and to hear lifesaving wisdom from people they might not listen to in their ordinary lives. When members who are not professionals see that qualifications in the outside world don't matter in NA, it sends the message that NA is a place where wisdom, experience, empathy, and humanity are valued more than anything else.

Our nonprofessional status frees us in many ways. We learn to show up, keep our commitments, and solve our differences. We learn how to learn. We don't need to worry whether we're good enough—we simply share our experience. NA can do what it does best and each of us can do what needs to be done. If we are honest, open-minded, and willing to ask for help, we can rise to any challenge. Like so many things in recovery, what matters is that we show up and do the work, to the best of our ability. The rest has a way of working itself out.

It's a funny thing to say, but in this anonymous Fellowship, all we have is our name. We come in without titles or associations, and come to know each other through our words and actions. Everything else that seems to matter outside of Narcotics Anonymous doesn't matter inside. Not only are we equal in membership "regardless of age, race, sexual identity, creed, religion, or lack of religion," but also regardless of social class, education, career, or credentials. Our bond as fellows begins and ends at one thing: We are addicts with a desire to stop using. We come to NA, and we bring our suffering with us. None of us arrives to NA at our best, but each of us finds that we have more to offer the world than we had ever imagined.

GROUP INVENTORY QUESTIONS

The questions below offer ways to begin—or continue—group inventory or discussion focused on this Tradition.

1. What do we mean by *nonprofessional*? How does this matter to our group?

2. Do people at our meeting give advice or feedback in response to what other addicts share, or do members focus on sharing their own experience?

3. If we sign court cards or otherwise verify attendance, how do we do so in a way that allows us to remain nonprofessional and nonaffiliated?

4. What are some strategies we can use to ensure that addicts feel safe sharing and a clear message is carried? How does our nonprofessional approach meet common challenges like a strong treatment presence, a lot of newcomers, or professionals attending with their clients?

5. How does our group respond when professionals, students, or others come to observe our meeting?

6. How does this Tradition help us understand anonymity? How does anonymity help us understand this Tradition? How do we practice anonymity in terms of this Tradition?

7. Discuss any bridges between this Tradition and other Traditions. What do these bridges teach us about our group?

8. What more can we do to bring the principles of this Tradition into our group efforts? What could we do differently to better fulfill our primary purpose?

In Service

Our nonprofessional approach to recovery is practiced in every NA community in the world. Service centers and special workers, on the other hand, are found in relatively few places in our Fellowship. When we hire or contract with someone for any task in NA, we understand that this is exceptional for us. We seek to define as clearly as we can what we are hiring them for, and what are the limits of that job. Special workers answer to NA service bodies, and they work within the guidance of our Traditions to carry out their tasks.

When we think of special workers, we may focus on the full-time staff at NA World Services, or we may consider the desk clerk, shipper, or office manager at the nearest NA service center. These are special workers—but what about the vendors at our conventions? What about the answering service we engage with to route our helpline calls? Many of the people we employ—or pay to do work for us in some way—are not employees and may not fit neatly under the label "special workers." Still, the guidance in Tradition Eight can be applied for those situations as well. We do not ask the vendors with whom we work to apply our Traditions, but we apply them ourselves as we consider the question, shape the relationship, and create a contract in which we can practice our principles when we engage in the commercial world. Hiring a special worker is not necessarily a "forever" commitment. We may hire a special worker to help us straighten out our financial records and then find that we can do the day-to-day bookkeeping on our own. Our needs, resources, and abilities fluctuate over time, and we adapt accordingly.

Our trusted servants are vital parts of our services at every level. Someone has to do the work of NA. Member volunteers and trusted servants, with the help of special workers, come together to serve NA. There are many different roles in service, and they ought never represent or create classes of membership. If we practice service as a part of our recovery, it is likely that we will serve in many different roles over time. Some of us never hold a service position at all—and again, our membership never depends on our involvement or lack of involvement.

Our trusted servants are responsible, and we often hold them to high standards for performance. Still, we do not treat our trusted servants as employees. Although service matters to the trusted servant and to the body, we still know that people have other priorities and that life sometimes intervenes. Our trusted servants tend to have jobs, families, or other parts of their lives outside NA that are important to them, just as their service to NA is. We often serve in our spare time, even when what we do in service feels like one of the most important things in our lives. Setting priorities among our many obligations is one of the most valuable, and difficult, things we do in service.

Stories of early members who made great personal sacrifices on behalf of NA are inspiring. Recovering addicts, inspired by the possibility of what NA could be, gave of themselves completely and made sacrifices that were truly heroic. That spirit is a part of who we are and how we came to be. There are still times and places where members give of themselves beyond reason or expectation. To expect or demand that level of commitment from all trusted servants would dishonor those who gave so much to build a foundation. That foundation allows us to recover in society, to build healthy lives and healthy NA communities. We respect our trusted servants, and understand that service is one part of our lives—and often not our only priority. Tradition Eight makes it possible to enlist the help of people beyond our volunteer trusted servants in order to get some of our work done. Special workers have a different type of responsibility and are held accountable in much more specific ways for their performance. Unlike trusted servants, whose obligations to NA are primarily spiritual in nature, special workers are obligated contractually. The formality of employment and compensation adds a measure of accountability to the work that is not always possible with trusted servants.

We don't hire professionals to do service for us, but rather to support our service efforts. For example, we may hire someone to record the meetings at our convention, print the T-shirts we sell, or audit our financial records to ensure that our accounting is adequate and accurate. Each time we make a decision to engage a paid worker, we do it with a clear understanding of the accountability, a fair rate of pay, the task at hand, and the limits of the job.

There is a distinction between employing a special worker and reimbursing trusted servants for service-related expenses. Reimbursement makes it possible for many of us to serve when travel or other expenses might limit service to those who could afford it. Payment to a special worker, on the other hand, is a fair rate for a specific job. We pay special workers for their time and expertise. Our commitment to self-support means not accepting outside contributions, and considering carefully what is appropriate to ask of our members. When a task is a priority for us and calls for significant expertise or time involvement, we seek out paid assistance and budget accordingly.

Any decision to hire a special worker should come after serious consideration and discussion by the service body. We consider our needs, our budget, and our plans. We determine what our process will be for hiring, firing, and contracting work. We think carefully about the tasks that will be assigned, how performance will be measured, and to whom our special workers will be accountable. Without a well-defined understanding of the job, the pay, and the structure within which the special worker operates, we are inviting problems down the road. Understanding the legal requirements that may apply, and knowing who will be accountable for meeting those requirements, is another matter that must be considered.

Special workers may have varying levels of input on the work that is done, but they remain accountable to NA service bodies. A special worker may be involved in a particular kind of service for much longer than the trusted servants around them; the institutional memory they carry might be vital to the decisions a body will make. The job of a special worker is to carry out the will of the service body to which they are assigned. Even if a special worker is a member, Tradition Eight clarifies that there are no professional recovering addicts in NA. Trusted servants and special workers work together to accomplish tasks, assist with Fellowship decision making, or help communities learn about NA and NA service, but do not share their personal recovery or sponsor people as part of their responsibilities. We are grateful for the work of our trusted servants, along with our special workers and the various vendors we do business with. Prudent use of these resources makes it possible for us to create an environment in NA where members are able to freely share recovery with one another. By doing what we can for ourselves and paying for help when necessary, we ensure that Narcotics Anonymous is able to remain forever nonprofessional.

WORKSHOP QUESTIONS

The questions below offer a way to begin—or continue—a service discussion or workshop focused on this Tradition.

1. What does being "forever nonprofessional" mean for our service efforts? Does that change the way we approach our work? How does that affect the ways we work with other organizations or the public?

2. Has our service body needed assistance from professionals or contract workers to complete a task or project? When would we consider hiring a special worker?

3. What tasks take too much specialization or time to ask volunteers to do? How do we balance our aspirations with our resources? If we are not able to hire outside assistance, what are our alternatives moving forward?

4. What can special workers do in NA? What work can't we hire special workers to do?

5. Have we had any interaction with a special worker? Why, and what was the outcome? What would be a reason to contact or visit an NA service office?

6. Why do some communities have service offices? What are the advantages/disadvantages of having one? Why would we decide to open—or close—a service office?

7. What responsibilities do we have to the special workers we employ? How do we fulfill those responsibilities?

8. What administrative needs would hiring special workers demand of us? Would we need legal or tax status to do so? Who would supervise, hire, and pay that worker? What additional bookkeeping would be required? Would having an employee be more work than doing the task ourselves?

9. Do we use contract workers or outside vendors at our conventions or events? What considerations are involved in doing so? Do we have standard practices in place for collecting bids or deciding who to contract with?

10. If our event or service body is making NA merchandise available, have we consulted the relevant service bulletins about the use of our logos and trademarks? Are we going about it in a way that is in harmony with the Fellowship's conscience?

11. How does membership in NA affect a special worker's relationship with the Traditions? If a special worker isn't a member, can the Traditions still apply?

12. What do we do if a well-meaning nonmember volunteers to perform a task for us, such as legal or financial services? At what point would this type of work constitute an outside contribution in terms of Tradition Seven? Does it make a difference if the individual is a family member of someone in NA?

13. How does this Tradition help us understand anonymity?
    How does anonymity help us understand this Tradition?
    How do we practice anonymity in terms of this Tradition?

14. Discuss any bridges between this Tradition and one or more of the Twelve Concepts. What do these bridges teach us about our service efforts?

15. What more can we do to bring the principles of this Tradition into our service efforts? What could we do differently to better carry out our services?

The guidance of our Traditions is simple: We are prudent with our funds and we pay fairly for what we need. We learn to practice discretion in how we select our services, and we recognize that perception is an important factor in avoiding conflicts of interest. The result is that we do not need to defend our relationships with other organizations, because practicing Traditions Six, Seven, and Eight together ensures our autonomy from any of the people or organizations that would be willing to use our name. It also protects us from being drawn into political or financial scandals and from any suspicion that we, on our own, are insufficient to carry our message. Insecurity puts us at risk. The Traditions keep us on track by reminding us that the spiritual principles we follow are more precious—and more powerful—than the seemingly attractive benefits that can so easily divert us.

Because there is no such thing as a professional NA member, we are all free to recover together, to learn from each other, and to practice anonymity. We demonstrate integrity in the respect we show to each other and to our special workers. In spite of challenges or disagreements that arise, we know that we all serve for the same reason: We love Narcotics Anonymous, and have a desire to help the addict who still suffers. We need no degrees, certifications, or training to carry the NA message—all we need is our experience, strength, and hope.

NA, as such, ought never be organized, but we may create service boards or committees directly responsible to those they serve.

TRADITION

9

NA is a spiritual program. Whatever boards and committees we create, however many meetings we hold, it's the spirit of NA that matters. We feel that spirit fill a room when we gather for a meeting, but it's not the room that matters. We carry NA with us, but it's bigger than we are.

When one addict helps another, NA is there. NA isn't one addict or the other; it's the helping, the sharing, the spirit of unity, the feeling of hope shared between us. When we read NA literature or listen to an addict share, we experience Narcotics Anonymous. When we write, when we pray, when we answer the phone even though we're tired or busy, or when we feel like using but we talk to another addict instead—that's NA. It's not just a thing; it's action. Chapter Ten in our Basic Text describes love as the "flow of life energy from one person to another." We offer it in meetings, at the "meeting after the meeting," on the phone, online, at our H&I panels, and in our literature. We share experience, strength, and hope to help one another stay clean one more day.

NA lives in our hearts, our minds, our spirits, and our actions. We are Narcotics Anonymous, and what we do—the empathy and care we show each other, the experience, strength, and hope we bring—that is "NA, as such."

NA is like the air we breathe; it surrounds us when we share recovery. It flows between us, constantly changing. We can no more keep recovery by holding it to ourselves than we could keep oxygen by holding our breath.

Tradition Nine

Our service efforts in Narcotics Anonymous help to make it possible for one addict to reach out to another. We began as a few addicts with hope, vision, and a willingness to serve. Today, NA meetings bring hope and help to addicts seeking recovery all over the world. What we have accomplished together is amazing. The fact that we have done it without being organized seems incredible, but in fact it is foundational. Our growth could not have happened without application of these principles.

Together, we do so much. We start meetings and keep the doors open. We carry the message into hospitals and institutions. We inform governments, agencies, and related professions what NA is and how we can help. We create newsletters and service materials that help us serve more effectively. We write and translate literature to ensure that the message we carry is true and consistent across time and distance. As we have grown, we have created service boards and committees in many different ways. Groups have come together to form service bodies that help them achieve their primary purpose. Service bodies have formed workgroups, boards, and committees to accomplish the tasks that support the groups.

We understand that "ought never be organized" doesn't mean that we do what we do without any planning or predictability. Our meetings are at regular times and places; we create and maintain meeting schedules, websites, and phonelines. In order for us to grow and recover, we need some structure. Administration is not the same as governance, and the structures we create in service are not the kind of organization this Tradition addresses. We absolutely organize our service efforts, our meeting schedules, and our event calendars. What is never organized is the part that matters most: one addict helping another, reaching out and sharing from heart to heart. The wordless language of empathy is what makes NA work. Without that, the rest of what we do would be meaningless.

We do not organize what people say; we do not choose who will reach out to whom, assign sponsors, mandate Step work, or insist that the Twelve Steps must be worked in one certain way. There is no certifying exam to qualify one addict to help another, we do not drug test each other, and our membership is not determined by the quantity or quality of work we do. We never know who will save our lives, or the life of another addict, or who will help an addict get the message or stay clean another day. Each of us shares our experience, strength, and hope in our own way, and the result is something bigger than any of us could manage or organize—it's the spirit of one addict helping another.

We can't organize our collective spirit; it's free. However, we can—and we must—ensure that that spirit has all it needs to thrive and grow. Chapter Two in our Basic Text tells us, "The heart of NA beats when two addicts share their recovery." That heartbeat is "NA, as such." The work we do in service to NA ought always be in a spirit of unity: We hold each other accountable, and we are responsible to those we serve, so that our personalities are less likely to divert us. The practice of being responsible to those we serve teaches us to surrender to the will of the group and have patience with the process. These skills serve us in our personal recovery and in our ongoing development as a Fellowship.

 ## WORD BY WORD

Define, expand on, or clarify the words or phrases from this Tradition, one at a time or in relation to each other, for writing or discussion with your sponsor or other NA members.

Example: responsible

We can understand the word *responsible* in a number of different ways, and each brings another understanding of Tradition Nine. Deriving from the root "to respond," the word implies communication. Being responsible means that we are accountable for our actions; it also means that we are able to respond to something coming from outside ourselves. Having a feeling is one kind of response; sharing that feeling is another kind. When we are responsible, we are both accountable and in communication. These two parts are especially important to us in NA, because our inclination is often to mistake responsibility for ownership or control—and no one of us owns any part of NA. We take care of it with each other, for each other, and for the addict still to come.

SPIRITUAL PRINCIPLES

Each Tradition embodies a variety of spiritual principles. The list of principles and values below may be useful as we consider applications of this Tradition. Explore them in writing or discussion with your sponsor or other NA members. If other principles or values not listed below seem relevant for you, include those as well.

- humility
- communication
- anonymity

- prudence
- trust
- simplicity

- fidelity
- harmony

- honesty
- love

Example: simplicity

When *It Works: How and Why* addresses spiritual principles in Tradition Nine, it begins with simplicity. Both our service and our thought about this Tradition should be simple. We start not from the sometimes complex relationship between service boards and groups, but instead with "NA, as such," the Fellowship of recovering addicts who help each other stay clean. When we start from here, the rest falls into place. The relationships between this Tradition and our First, our Fifth, and certainly our Twelfth all become evident. Unity and anonymity allow us to carry our message without getting distracted by personalities. When our service is simple and uncluttered, we can stay focused on our primary purpose. It is easy to see the connections between our work and the suffering addict.

For Members

As individual members, our relationship to Tradition Nine develops in two ways: in what it has to teach us about our personal lives, and in the guidance it offers for how we serve. Our willingness to take responsibility for our Fellowship is not separate from our practice of taking responsibility for our own lives.

Practicing the Traditions teaches us balance. Tradition Seven encourages us to be self-supporting; Tradition Eight reminds us that total self-reliance can be a defect and encourages us to seek assistance when we need it. Tradition Nine cautions that while we may need assistance, we don't get to walk away after we ask for it.

We balance between asking for help and ensuring that the work is done according to plan. We balance between maintaining our responsibility and allowing service boards and committees to carry out the tasks assigned to them. We give our trusted servants room to carry out their tasks, and we also keep ourselves informed enough to ensure that the work stays on course and there are enough members involved to get it done.

Allowing others to have input can improve our work many times over. It takes patience and open-mindedness to be able to listen to feedback, but the process is almost always worth the time. Even if it results in no change to our practice, we gain a deeper understanding of the principles involved. Almost always, however, opening a process to input changes the result for the better.

Some of us come into recovery with no sense of personal responsibility, as if it was someone else's job to take care of us. Others of us experience self-obsession as a belief that we are responsible for everything around us. The reality is usually somewhere in between. We find peace of mind when we are able to trust others to carry out responsibilities without constantly looking over their shoulders, and they show the same courtesy to us.

Service can be joyful and exciting. It feels good to do good. We learn and grow in service, and our lives are enriched by the relationships we build there. Yet we are always responsible to those we serve. It may be that we serve our home group, or the area, or another service body. It is up to us to understand who we serve and to whom we are accountable. Whatever task we are doing, we can ask, what body am I serving? And then, what body does that body serve? And so on, until ultimately the answer takes us back to the group, and from there to the addict who still suffers and our Higher

Power. In between, we should be able to see a clear line of accountability. That helps us to understand our role in the process.

Loving service is the work of a Power greater than ourselves. The privilege to participate in the miracle does not make us miracle workers. Tradition Nine helps us to retain our anonymity even as we help to accomplish great things, because it reminds us that we are always servants. Whatever our service efforts, we are guided by our sense of responsibility to the addict who still suffers, and by the direction of those who care enough to stay informed and involved.

Without other people to discuss our plans with, it's much easier to run off course. We may encounter trouble when service responsibilities are one-member operations. When we act alone, we make decisions alone, and it's hard not to feel an ego investment in those decisions. NA service never happens in a vacuum; even when we seem to be by ourselves, there are no solo efforts in Narcotics Anonymous. Our direct responsibility to those we serve keeps us from falling victim to our own egos. It can be very difficult not to hear feedback as personal criticism.

When we communicate openly, we invite discussion, and as we discuss, we often find better ways to do things than any one of us had imagined. In order for a discussion to get us to a new place, we need to let go of our attachment to one particular answer. Being able to track lines of accountability helps us to see the connection between responsibility and surrender. That, in turn, helps to free us from the traps of isolation, resentment, and suspicion that can divide us from one another. Open and clear communication helps us to achieve and maintain accountability in service.

Early in the process we begin to learn the difference between freedom *from* and freedom *to*. Freedom *from* active addiction begins with not using today. That, in turn, gives us freedom *to* experience a new way of life, which may take us places we had never dreamed of or restore dreams we had lost long ago. In much the same way, we find that responsibility *for* something is different from responsibility *to*. We are responsible *for* the task assigned to us; we are responsible *to* the body we report to. In our services, these two are equally important. All the service we do involves accountability *to* and *for* NA, and accountability doesn't just keep us honest; it keeps us connected to the group conscience and our Higher Power. It can be easy to mistake self-will for a driving need. Surrender to group conscience doesn't disempower us; it reminds us to keep service separate from our ego, and frees us from any illusions that service experience or outcomes somehow affect our value as members. Serving in a spirit of selflessness and humility can be challenging, but it's good for us and good for the service we do. That process of surrender will drive us to the Steps—probably more than once.

QUESTIONS FOR MEMBERS

The questions below offer a way to begin—or continue—the process of writing, reflection, and discussion of this Tradition with your sponsor or other NA members.

IN NA

1. When do I most feel like a part of NA, as such? What actions help me to experience that feeling?

2. How do I practice responsibility as a member and a servant? To whom am I responsible in any service positions I currently hold? To whom am I responsible when I perform service without a title?

3. How do I balance accountability, responsibility, and authority in my NA service positions? How do I determine when it's best to seek guidance from those I serve and when it's appropriate to exercise the trust placed in me as a trusted servant?

4. How do I know when to serve and when to step away? What happens when I try to run things in NA? When have I struggled to step out of a service position gracefully?

5. How do I determine what needs to be communicated to my group or between levels of service? Where do I turn for reliable information?

6. What are some examples of effective communication in service? How can I make my communication more interesting and understandable? What has NA service taught me about listening?

7. How does this Tradition help me understand anonymity? How does anonymity help me understand this Tradition? How do I practice anonymity in terms of this Tradition?

8. Describe any bridges between this Tradition and one or more of the Twelve Steps. What do these bridges teach me about my recovery?

9. What more can I do to put the principles of this Tradition into action? How would applying this Tradition change my attitudes and actions?

IN ALL OUR AFFAIRS

10. How have I applied this Tradition outside NA? How else might the principles of this Tradition guide my thinking or my actions?

11. How do I take responsibility for my actions while practicing surrender about outcomes?

12. How easy is it for me to ask for and accept feedback? What is my response to constructive criticism?

13. When someone asks me for an opinion, how do I respond? Am I kind? Do I feel like I have to find something to correct? Do I point out something positive when I offer criticism?

14. Are there areas of my life that would benefit from more planning? Do I do better with more or less structure in my life? Do I resist routine or embrace it?

15. How do I create structure and predictability in my life without being rigid or controlling? Can I plan for the future if I'm living just for today?

16. How would I describe the spirit of service? What would it mean for me to embrace that spirit in all my affairs?

17. Do I find it easier to handle tasks on my own when it might be beneficial to include others? Are there things I'm taking care of myself that should be done with other members of my household, community, or work environment?

For Groups

There are at least two ways Tradition Nine offers guidance to our groups, both in how the group operates and in the relationship between the group and the boards and committees responsible to it.

NA, as such, ought never be organized. However, our groups have formats; we elect trusted servants; we have business meetings to handle matters that keep the group functioning and connected to NA as a whole. These are ways of being organized—our groups *are* organized. Our services need to be structured, and our bills paid; much of what we do in NA requires organization. However, the organizing we do to keep things functioning smoothly and predictably is not organizing "NA, as such." Groups don't tell people what to say to carry the message, or what is the only way to recover. Our groups create space for an unstructured, undefined thing to happen: One addict helps another by freely sharing experience, strength, and hope. We apply our Steps and Traditions in countless ways, and there are as many styles of recovery in NA as there are members. There are no professional NA members. We are all equal in NA, and all equally able to carry a message from our first day clean. In our recovery meetings, we make room for each other and for the magic that happens when we share recovery. Outside of meetings, we reach out to one another in ways that aren't structured. Our groups create an atmosphere of recovery; what happens inside that atmosphere is bigger than us. We don't get to control it.

In order for the group to practice its primary purpose, it needs to be focused on the message of recovery. Creating an atmosphere of recovery is a big job. To stay focused on that job, groups turn over most other tasks to service boards and committees—to ensure that the work gets done without diverting NA groups from their primary purpose.

Group responsibility does not end at creating boards and committees. Tradition Nine tells us that boards and committees are directly responsible to those they serve. Groups have a responsibility to be attentive to our service bodies. We can only be responsible if we are involved. If our boards and committees are responsible to us as groups, then we are responsible to pay attention to what they are doing. It's up to us to see that they know what is expected, and to ensure that there are NA members there to serve on that committee. We choose trusted servants to help communicate between each group and the rest of NA. Those members are responsible for bringing us accurate, timely information including reports, emails, flyers, local newsletters and websites, and so on. As a group, we are responsible for helping our trusted servants learn to do their jobs effectively.

When trusted servants are excited about service, we can feel it. When those we serve are grateful, we want to do more. Direct responsibility doesn't mean we look for reasons to criticize. We share responsibility when we participate, when we help each other to serve effectively, and when we acknowledge each other's efforts. Accountability is important, but so is celebration.

In places where only a few NA members have much cleantime, it can be easy to mistake experience for authority. In the same way, when a few groups actively participate, we can mistake them for "the groups that run things around here." No single member is more important than any other, nor does any single group have a greater say than others. This can be hard to remember when one or a few members are much more involved and informed than others. We can confuse the need for accountability with a belief that our group alone dictates to service committees what they should do. We are responsible to those we serve, not to those who serve most or speak loudest.

Every NA group participates in its own way. NA groups are autonomous, and our service bodies answer to the groups, not the other way around. Some members will do more service than others; some groups will be more involved than others; some communities will be more active than others. When we are present at the creation of service boards or committees, our sense of responsibility may be different from when we join a fully operational service body. Each of us has a part in our services, and all of us together create the conscience of our groups and our Fellowship.

While some of our service entities have been created by the groups, others have been created within service bodies themselves. Groups support and maintain local services. We create an area service committee, and that, in turn, creates subcommittees. Or the groups create a local service conference, and that creates workgroups to get things done. In either case, the tasks that emerge over time may grow far beyond what the groups originally envisioned. We need methods to communicate, challenge, consent to, and change our plans. Those systems may look very different from place to place, but the question we ask in our groups is whether it's working. If we remain flexible in our approach to carrying out our services, our services can continue to meet our needs and circumstances.

Communication is key to this Tradition. Any breakdown in the process ought to lead us to look at how we are communicating. As in any inventory, we look for our part. Sometimes, our groups have lost interest or felt disenfranchised by service matters. Other times, groups find it difficult to adequately participate due to distance or lack of time and other resources. Communication needs to be clear and interesting to make it attractive. Asking if a new member will understand what we are saying when we make an announcement will help us to consider how to get people excited about service. When service is exciting to us, it is naturally attractive to others.

The first three Concepts speak to the nature of NA services in the same way Tradition Nine does. Our groups join together to create services, and the final responsibility and authority rest with the NA groups. That we have so many reminders leading back to this same point indicates two things: one, that our groups are the heart of NA, and two, that we forget that a lot. We wouldn't need to repeat it so much if this were easy for us. For the groups to retain their focus on the primary purpose and to be able to exercise the authority vested in them, group members must be willing to devote time, energy, and thought to learning about NA and participating in decision making, however that occurs in our community. Being involved with local service is a choice for some groups and a challenge for others. Still, we look for ways to participate, support the services that further our message, and hold our service bodies accountable. Tradition Nine ensures that the groups always have a voice in our services.

GROUP INVENTORY QUESTIONS

The questions below offer ways to begin—or continue—group inventory or discussion focused on this Tradition.

1. How do we understand the phrase "NA, as such"? How does our group's understanding of "NA, as such" affect our actions or decisions as a group?

2. As a group, which aspects of our work together are organized, and which happen organically? Do we engage in any planning? Are our planning practices adequate for our group's needs?

3. How do we understand the roles of our trusted servants? Do we have positions for most tasks, or are they completed in a more informal manner?

4. Which of our trusted servants help us to stay connected to the larger NA community? How does this connection help to provide communication and accountability?

5. Why have we created boards or committees? How do we practice responsibility for the boards or committees we create?

6. How does this Tradition help us understand anonymity? How does anonymity help us understand this Tradition? How do we practice anonymity in terms of this Tradition?

7. Discuss any bridges between this Tradition and other Traditions. What do these bridges teach us about our group?

8. What more can we do to bring the principles of this Tradition into our group efforts? What could we do differently to better fulfill our primary purpose?

In Service

Tradition Nine speaks directly about our service bodies, and this Tradition is vital to understanding how we serve in Narcotics Anonymous. Traditions Seven, Eight, and Nine together remind us who we are and what we are: a Fellowship of addicts seeking recovery. We are not a school, a business, a treatment center, or a governmental agency. NA is nonprofessional, as indicated by Tradition Eight, and ought never be organized—but that doesn't mean we're thoughtless and disorganized. We create service bodies that do business on our behalf, but they are always a part of Narcotics Anonymous. They are responsible to those they serve, and that responsibility ought always determine what we do and how we do it.

Being directly responsible may sometimes seem inefficient or inconvenient, but some things are more important than efficiency. As addicts, most of us are familiar with living in a perpetual state of emergency, and it can be too easy to operate this way in service. The sense of desperate urgency—we have to do it right now, we have to fix it right now, or we need to raise funds right now—is a sign that we are running on fear rather than hope. Our perception of our circumstances doesn't just determine how we feel; it changes how we respond to the world around us. When we are compelled by fear and desperation, we are not likely to make our best decisions.

The relationship between our groups and NA services is much more than a two-way street; it's an elaborate web. Autonomous groups have relationships with each other, service boards and committees have relationships with the groups, and boards and committees are in relationship and communication with each other. The web is made up of many strands and connections, and making sure those threads remain strong begins when we ensure that there is a free flow of information, support, and goodwill.

When we are deep in a service project, we may develop a close working relationship with others on the project. H&I can sometimes feel like its own tribe, for example, or a convention committee may come together like a family. When we get through all the difficulty of developing a working committee, when consensus develops and the way forward seems clear—it can feel inconvenient or even wrong to have to consult those outside the little group. Service bodies can feel separate from those they serve. But responsibility doesn't work without communication, and sometimes we have to explain our decisions and accept input; we may even be redirected in ways that are hard for the committee to accept. Direct responsibility to those we serve means that those we serve have a voice in what we do, wherever or however we serve. Constructive criticism sometimes feels like just plain criticism, but if we set aside our feelings and listen closely, the input may improve our service efforts.

Finding the balance between ensuring that our service boards are responsible and allowing a minority of onlookers to micromanage or bully our trusted servants can be harder than it sounds. A small number of people or groups may have very strong feelings about an issue that has already been settled. Resolving these differences without bitterness is challenging, and requires that we listen carefully to each other. Small changes can often resolve big issues if we can listen for the principles behind a problem. Direct responsibility thrives on mutual respect and unity. Even when we have very different ideas of how to get there, we are working together toward the same primary purpose. Our commitment to unity and goodwill keeps us involved even when we don't agree.

Service efforts are enriched by active involvement. When it's not just the same few people doing most of the work, when there's rotation of trusted servants and new people are getting involved, service is dynamic and exciting. Otherwise, service bodies can start to feel closed. New people feel like they're interrupting, or unwelcome. We resist new ideas or new ways of doing things. Complacency can kill an NA community in much the same way it can kill an addict: The spark goes out of our recovery, and gradually we forget it was ever there.

While "those we serve" in this Tradition ultimately refers to the NA groups, we may want to consider some other layers of responsibility we experience in NA service, and be mindful of what it means to be directly responsible to, and through, our levels of service. A hospitality committee may be responsible to the convention committee, for example; the convention committee answers directly to the hosting service body; RCMs report back to the areas, and so our groups are informed and able to be responsible. Because there are so many layers, we need to think carefully about what must be communicated and how to get that information to and from our points of responsibility. Each has a part to play in the work at hand, and yet the work must go forward in a way that is timely—and, yes, organized.

We recognize that some issues really need to go back to the groups, but sometimes the groups will attend to an issue that a committee hadn't seen as important, or had been decided long ago. Allowing everyone into the process means that we need to be able to explain how and why decisions were made without becoming impatient or intolerant of those who are asking. Even so, when an issue has been raised and decided many times already, it may not be prudent to revisit decisions if the circumstances and information haven't changed much.

Concept Five gives us tools to more effectively practice Tradition Nine: Clear lines of accountability and decision making draw clear lines of communication between our boards and committees and those we serve. Our groups always hold the reins on our service bodies—not the other way around. No single group is responsible for our service boards; our service boards do not manage or oversee our groups. Groups, not service bodies, are autonomous.

Direct responsibility is difficult. It's a practical principle that requires spiritual effort. The relationship between our groups and our service bodies changes over time and differs from one place to another. Our widespread growth and development is a testament to the value of our flexibility and reliance on the simple guidance offered by our Traditions. Our commitments to avoid professionalization, organization, affiliation, and outside support keep us free to do what we do best regardless of changes in fashion or politics. Tradition Nine helps us practice anonymity by keeping us from creating structures that would make us unequal. We practice mentorship and train our trusted servants in a spirit of rotation and continuity. Whatever our lives or circumstances are like, in Narcotics Anonymous we all have a voice in the process and an opportunity to serve. Our service helps others every day, and each of us who serves finds our own recovery enriched by the work. It drives us to learn, to grow, to practice principles, and to reach out in new directions. Tradition Nine reminds us that we are never doing this alone. Our service efforts are always guided and supported by our groups and by that greater conscience that guides us all.

WORKSHOP QUESTIONS _____

The questions below offer a way to begin—or continue—a service discussion or workshop focused on this Tradition.

1. What functions does this service body accomplish on behalf of the groups? How do we get input from groups as we plan? How can we maintain effective communication between groups and their boards or committees?

2. What role do collaboration and communication play in helping us to create NA unity?

3. What is the meaning of the term *directly* as it relates to Tradition Nine? How does the "direct" link help us to maintain responsibility? How does this body remain directly responsible to those we serve?

4. How do our needs change in times of rapid growth? Are we growing now, or have we hit a plateau? How can our service efforts help us grow in ways that are sustainable for us?

5. Have we noticed occasions when our services need to be more organized than they were, or when our efforts have become too structured?

6. How do we balance our needs for both rotation and continuity? What are our practices regarding training, support, and mentorship? Are we willing to leave a service position open rather than electing a member who is not well suited to the role?

7. How does this Tradition help us understand anonymity? How does anonymity help us understand this Tradition? How do we practice anonymity in terms of this Tradition?

8. Discuss any bridges between this Tradition and one or more of the Twelve Concepts. What do these bridges teach us about our service efforts?

9. What more can we do to bring the principles of this Tradition into our service efforts? What could we do differently to better carry out our services?

Direct responsibility is a critical concept in our lives and in service. It's not just that we are accountable for the work we do; we stay aware of what we are doing, why we are doing it, and who will benefit from our efforts. This clarity keeps us from being diverted or distracted by our egos, or by arguments over territory or control. Narcotics Anonymous belongs to all of us, and it is too easy to mistake our desires and opinions for those of the Fellowship as a whole. Being directly responsible keeps us on track and in proportion.

Tradition Nine reminds us where our service bodies fit within NA as a whole. Our service boards and committees are always ultimately responsible to those they serve. In our efforts to practice this Tradition, each of us can learn to communicate more effectively and to practice principles including honesty, patience, and accountability. Tradition Nine helps us to keep our primary purpose constantly in mind as we serve.

Narcotics Anonymous has no opinion on outside issues; hence the NA name ought never be drawn into public controversy.

TRADITION

10

As our thinking becomes clearer, our ability to be honest increases. Honesty begins with not lying, but that's not where it ends. We start to recognize the difference between what's true for us and what sounds good—or what we wish was true. We don't have to argue about practices or politics. Recovery is no longer based in theory; it's our own experience. The better we get at telling the truth, the clearer our message becomes.

We know that anything that affects our recovery is material for sharing, but finding the message in the raw material of our lives can be challenging. When we share in meetings, it helps if we look for a connection to the topic, to a Step, a Tradition, or another recovery principle. Sharing can help us look for solutions, which is part of how sharing helps us. Finding the message in our experience helps us to understand its exact nature.

We experience unity when we hear our story from a member who seems so different from us. Our shared experience as recovering addicts is stronger than any of the forces that could divide us. That connection is the heartbeat of NA, and evidence of a Higher Power working in our meetings.

Our experience, strength, and hope carry a clearer message than our opinions ever could. Sharing from the heart connects us to our common experience and common purpose.

Tradition Ten

Clarity and simplicity are keys to our message. Tradition Ten is clear and simple, as well. Narcotics Anonymous, all by itself, is enough. We promise freedom from active addiction. We don't take positions on outside issues, and we don't allow the NA name to be drawn into controversy.

NA is a program of complete abstinence, and it works in the lives of countless addicts around the world. Recovery is possible for any addict who chooses to follow our way. Still, our way is not the only way, and we don't even have an opinion on whether it is the best way. The NA way is the only approach on which we have an opinion. We know it works for those who want what we have and are willing to make the effort to get it.

Some of the principles that are central to our program are not universally shared outside NA. Our belief in total abstinence is viewed by some as extreme. Some disagree with our commitment to personal anonymity. These principles are not negotiable—and we do not have to debate them. We may want to defend our name or explain our position, but we don't need to. We don't need to argue that NA is the best or the only way to recover; what matters is that it works for us.

The language of this Tradition points to two ways we can find ourselves in the storm of public opinion: by taking a position ourselves, or by being drawn into public controversy by someone else. There are issues closely related to our primary purpose that may feel urgent—it might seem like we should take a position on public policy or trends in addiction treatment, but in fact these things have nothing to do with Narcotics Anonymous. The *PR Handbook* offers guidance on how we practice Tradition Ten in a presentation or H&I meeting: "The only way we can be drawn into public controversy is if we offer an opinion on an issue outside the scope of our own program." When we get tangled up in argument, we risk being drawn into positions that will compromise us in some other way. Rather than taking positions on issues that are none of our business, we talk about NA and then stop. Our message speaks for itself; our success is defense enough. Many of us are drawn to an interesting or heated debate, but Tradition Ten requires that we let it go by. We are responsible for keeping our focus.

Engaging in debate with those whose approach differs from ours, or with those who criticize our program, would distract us from our primary purpose and risk alienating the newcomer. We don't need to invest energy or interest in the conversations that swirl around us. We know our message and our purpose. We do what we do. Focusing on our primary purpose frees us from the need to be distracted or diverted into debates with those whose interests and motives differ. No one outside NA is under any obligation to respect our Traditions. Our commitments to unity, anonymity, and our primary purpose are ours alone.

Drawn directly from the experiences of those who went before us, Tradition Ten serves as a guidepost and a warning. One early addiction recovery movement grew to thousands of members, until some of its leaders began speaking for the organization on a number of political issues. As the group started taking public positions on issues other than recovery, membership fell away, and they were soon forgotten. Throughout the history of NA, a number of fledgling NA communities have faced difficulties or collapse because of promotion, publicity, and controversy. Our commitment never to draw the NA name into public controversy is a matter of survival for the Fellowship we love, and for all of us addicts who need Narcotics Anonymous.

The lines between NA and the outside world are often clearer than the lines between our personal lives and our membership in NA. It can be difficult to see where our relationship with NA ends and our outside interests begin. If we have a religious or spiritual practice outside NA that matters deeply to us, we may feel very little distance between our experience on that path and "practicing these principles in all our affairs." Or, if we work in treatment, we may be addressing suffering addicts all day long before we come to a meeting. Still, what we do in NA is different. Recognizing and honoring that difference is critical to our integrity as a Fellowship and to our personal recovery.

We don't live outside of history. Our recovery and our Fellowship exist against a backdrop of real events and issues that sometimes affect us profoundly. Outside issues that appear to intersect with our purpose or message almost invite us to take a position. Our ability to rise above in these moments protects us from debates that would tear us apart.

WORD BY WORD

Define, expand on, or clarify the words or phrases from this Tradition, one at a time or in relation to each other, for writing or discussion with your sponsor or other NA members.

Example: controversy

In general, a *controversy* is a disagreement in which there are strong opposing views. Some say a dispute needs to be public, prolonged, and polarizing in order to be considered a controversy. We immediately see the danger, as well as the attraction. Controversy is interesting, and we like a contest. The prospect of winning or losing can become more important to us than the idea over which we are fighting. We often see this pattern in our personal relationships as well as in service. Keeping our Fellowship out of public controversy protects us from ourselves: We cannot afford to risk our reputation or the well-being of our members over an issue not directly related to our primary purpose. The root words of *controversy* mean "to turn against," so it's easy to see the challenge controversy presents us in NA. What can we turn against without affecting our unity?

SPIRITUAL PRINCIPLES

Each Tradition embodies a variety of spiritual principles. The list of principles and values below may be useful as we consider applications of this Tradition. Explore them in writing or discussion with your sponsor or other NA members. If other principles or values not listed below seem relevant for you, include those as well.

• humility	• unity	• responsibility	• prudence
• anonymity	• integrity	• discernment	• fidelity
• simplicity	• freedom	• caution	• patience
• tolerance	• acceptance		

Example: fidelity and integrity

When we practice fidelity we are also practicing integrity. We are consistent, true to our message, and faithful to our purpose. Integrity suggests that we are acting in accordance with our beliefs and values—we are not just sharing clean, we are living clean. Fidelity suggests that we are true and faithful to our message, that it is consistent on all occasions. When we practice these principles together, it is virtually impossible for us to engage in controversy. When we are stuck in an argument we can't seem to resolve, it may be useful to consider how fidelity and integrity can help us to get back on course.

For Members

Narcotics Anonymous has no opinion on outside issues. As members we do, and each of us has a right to our opinions, although a recovery meeting is usually not the best place to discuss them. In recovery, we get to think for ourselves. As we work the Steps, we come to an understanding of our own morals and values, and develop our own beliefs about how to live and how we recover. Those beliefs may change over time, sometimes surprisingly. Recovery is a dynamic process of evaluation and reevaluation of our actions, perceptions, and values. Tradition Ten asks us to be vigilant in ensuring that our personal beliefs aren't mistaken for principles of Narcotics Anonymous. We carefully consider the effect our words and actions may have on the Fellowship we love and the message we carry. We learn to speak wisely and to understand the power of silence.

Though we express it in many ways, NA has only one message: "An addict, any addict, can stop using drugs, lose the desire to use, and find a new way to live." When we hear another message outside NA that resonates strongly with us, it may seem that we could do a service by bringing it to our fellow members. That is not our purpose in an NA meeting. We are here to help and be helped through the program of Narcotics Anonymous.

We don't all know how to share a recovery message when we get here. If we have experience with some kinds of counseling or therapy, we may be inclined to offer advice to other members, but in NA we share experience, not advice. The ways we share with one another are different from the ways many of us communicated before coming to NA. We learn to share through each other's example and guidance, not by being bullied or humiliated. As we continue to share, we get more comfortable with the process of sorting out what feels appropriate to us.

Exploring our motives for sharing and asking ourselves what it is that we bring to the meeting can help guide us away from diversion or controversy. We may need to share about what's going on, but we try to stay focused. Many of us struggle to share without getting tangled up in details, especially when our feelings are strong. "A guy shared that his political work was tearing him up," one member recounted, "but he never mentioned which party he was from." Another suggested, "When I'm having a hard time keeping what I share to the topic of recovery, it's usually a sign that I need to get back into my Step work."

We don't always share an elegant, tidy message, and we don't rate or police each other's sharing. Many members connect with raw, emotional expression, while others may relate to a quiet, thoughtful share. Sharing in a meeting is both personal and courageous, no matter what we share. There is no such thing as sharing perfectly. Each of us struggles sometimes to get to the heart of the matter or to find a message of hope in our experience, and that struggle is part of the process for us. Placing unity first and anonymity at our foundation allows the message to shine through, even in the most awkward moments of a meeting.

Clarity, focus, and discretion are all assets that make our message attractive and effective. Even members who have been around a while can find it challenging to separate opinions from experience, but we try to be aware of that task. Sharing about a Higher Power without mentioning a name, sharing about our experience without identifying other people, institutions, or beliefs: These are skills we develop over time, and with some help. The ability to share clearly even when we are passionate about something is a message in itself.

NA has no opinion on human nature, but it seems that addicts are not the only people vulnerable to ego inflation. Winning an argument, being recognized as special, making a name for ourselves in the world, feeling loved and approved of—all these are positive experiences that almost anyone might be tempted to seek. But they carry a special risk for us. As we recover, many of us go forth into the world with renewed confidence in ourselves and our beliefs. That is beautiful, but it's essential that we leave NA out of it. Traditions Ten and Eleven remind us not to try to leverage membership into fame or fortune, power, or public approval. Anonymity is no small thing; it is the foundation of our Traditions, essential to our new way of life.

On the internet, and especially on social media, different aspects of our lives and beliefs can be visible in surprising ways. Our challenge is keeping the NA message separate from the other messages we may carry. If we are not vigilant in our privacy practices, we may discover that we are engaging in controversy—or being drawn in—as members of NA in ways that don't serve us or the Fellowship. The service pamphlet *Social Media and Our Guiding Principles* offers guidance on practicing the Traditions in our actions and behaviors online.

In so many ways, Tradition Ten is about wisdom. We learn when to speak the truth, and when silence is the wiser choice. When we feel we need to defend or explain, it's often because we are still not quite sure. "The wisdom to know the difference" that comes from practicing this Tradition in NA helps us in our work lives and our personal lives as well. We practice honesty and discretion, focus on the purpose at hand, and are not diverted by side topics or invitations to argument. We learn what is true for us and stand firm in that truth. The most effective approach may be to let go and let a challenge go by unaddressed. We can move mountains in recovery, but we don't have to move every mountain. Tradition Ten frees us to mind our own business. Being able to distinguish between necessary conflict and needless controversy frees us to direct our efforts where they can do the most good.

We share about our lives in ways that highlight our experiences rather than our opinions. When we interact with the public on behalf of NA, we refrain from speaking on any issue that doesn't relate to who we are and what we do as a Fellowship. We let go of our investment in other people's opinions. One member commented, "I practice this Tradition by remembering that *your* thoughts and opinions are outside issues to *me*." Practicing this personally helps us choose our battles, focus our efforts, and walk away from challenges with dignity.

QUESTIONS FOR MEMBERS

The questions below offer a way to begin—or continue—the process of writing, reflection, and discussion of this Tradition with your sponsor or other NA members.

IN NA

1. What issues does NA have an opinion on? What do I understand NA's opinion to be? What is the difference between sharing my opinion and sharing my experience?

2. What are some ways my opinions on outside issues affect my participation in NA? Do those beliefs affect the ways I sponsor, or participate in events? How do I balance strong opinions with the need to carry a clear message?

3. What would constitute an "outside issue" for NA? When I'm affected by such an issue, how can I share about it in a way that honors Tradition Ten? Have outside issues ever created conflict or disunity for me inside the rooms?

4. Have I had disagreements with other NA members about issues that seem to be affecting NA? What is the difference between public controversy and internal debate? How do I keep my opinions from reflecting on NA as whole?

5. When does controversy within the Fellowship start to feel like public controversy? What do I do when disagreements within NA feel intense or unsolvable? How do I avoid judgment and isolation?

6. Do I use my NA membership to gain credibility or authority in debates on outside issues? How can I avoid entangling the NA name in controversy, especially in my use of social media?

7. How does this Tradition help me understand anonymity? How does anonymity help me understand this Tradition? How do I practice anonymity in terms of this Tradition?

8. Describe any bridges between this Tradition and one or more of the Twelve Steps. What do these bridges teach me about my recovery?

9. What more can I do to put the principles of this Tradition into action? How would applying this Tradition change my attitudes and actions?

IN ALL OUR AFFAIRS

10. How have I applied this Tradition outside NA? How else might the principles of this Tradition guide my thinking or my actions?

11. What constitutes inside issues in other areas of my life? How do I determine which issues are and are not relevant in various areas of my life?

12. What value is there for me in setting aside controversial matters in my workplace, family, or elsewhere?

13. When have I taken a position on a subject I meant to stay neutral on? What drew me into controversy in that situation? Are there particular kinds of situations in which it's hard for me to remain neutral?

14. When have issues that seemed unimportant spiraled into conflict? What do those situations, in and out of NA, have in common?

For Groups

Tradition Ten reminds us that our groups do best when we allow NA—the simple way that has been proving itself in the lives of many addicts—to shine. Diversion, distraction, and controversy cloud our message and make it difficult to carry out our purpose. Integrity, clarity, and simplicity free us.

The group is the front line for our primary purpose. It is also a place where we can be easily distracted or disrupted. Creating an atmosphere of recovery is no easy task—but once that atmosphere exists, the job of protecting it is not that difficult. In much the same way that it's easier to keep a clean house tidy than to make a dirty house clean, when we maintain an atmosphere of recovery in a spirit of unity and goodwill, we can readily come back to the message after a momentary disruption.

We protect the atmosphere of recovery, but that doesn't mean we need to protect ourselves from everything shared by every member. There is a difference between a group expressing an opinion and a member sharing experience. The group can carry a clear message even when someone shares about an outside issue or attempts to create controversy. Our automatic response may be to want to debate or correct, but it is so much more powerful when we simply bring the sharing back around to what is important in NA, and keep it there.

Groups that continually struggle with outside issues being brought in may benefit from adding a statement to the meeting format, having literature study as part of the format, discussing rather than simply reading the Traditions, or offering meetings or workshops on our primary purpose. Members don't automatically know how to carry a clear message; we need guidance more than scolding, which might do more harm to the atmosphere of recovery than the initial share.

In our group business meetings, we make decisions about how the meeting will run, and other internal matters. Ensuring that those choices support our primary purpose rather than feeding disunity is a matter for group conscience. When outside issues creep in or cause problems, our first impulse may be to try to exert control by trying to ban a topic, enforce language norms, or set and announce a position in the group format. When we back away from the impulse to control, we can seek a solution based in principle that enhances unity, rather than enforcing uniformity. Practical decisions of the group are also spiritual, and often reflect back on NA as a whole.

Some groups hold workshops or newcomer meetings. Other groups have language in their meeting format that can help members consider how to respect the Twelve Traditions when they share. As a group, it's our job to be tolerant, listen well, hear the message through the mess, and encourage newer members to grow. The heart we put into sharing is often much more important than the words. Membership is not conditional on proper form, and no one member speaks for Narcotics Anonymous.

Addicts tend to be pretty skeptical. Trust doesn't come easily to us. We look for the thing that isn't true, or the thing that makes it impossible for us to recover. One by one, the Traditions address our reservations: We don't have to be a particular kind of person; we don't have to be a certain type of member to be equal as a member; we don't have authorities; we're not dependent on or affiliated with other organizations. Above all, NA is a program of attraction. Honoring our Traditions makes us attractive as a Fellowship. Tradition Ten keeps us focused and clean—clarity and simplicity, and our willingness to decline invitations to controversy, speak volumes for our integrity. We know what we stand for.

We want the NA name to be free of controversy, and our Traditions help us to stay true to ourselves. We don't promote our program; we don't defend our way of life; we don't use NA to make a point in some other argument. Expressing an opinion on an outside issue puts NA's name at risk and may alienate those who hold different views on those issues. Putting a member's identity alongside the NA name could have the same effect.

The relationship between Traditions Six and Ten is so close that we can hardly talk about one without the other. Tradition Six reminds us not to endorse or affiliate with others outside of NA, and Tradition Ten takes us to the next level, keeping our opinions on issues as well as organizations to ourselves. Traditions Six and Ten, along with Tradition Eleven, together ask us to seek stillness. When we decline to take a position on an issue, we practice anonymity and humility. Our only opinion is that NA works, and that is the message we carry in our groups—nothing more, nothing less.

GROUP INVENTORY QUESTIONS _____

The questions below offer ways to begin—or continue—group inventory or discussion focused on this Tradition.

1. How does our group understand the difference between an "outside" issue and an "inside" issue? Does our understanding show up in how our meetings function?

2. How do we stay focused on our primary purpose when non-NA issues affect our members and membership?

3. When our group seems pressed to form an opinion on an outside issue, how do we stay focused on our primary purpose?

4. If a member brings in an outside issue, what are some ways we can respond that avoid escalating controversy or alienating group members?

5. When we recognize that the group has been drawn into outside controversy, how do we regain our focus? What can we do to restore our atmosphere of recovery?

6. How does this Tradition help us understand anonymity? How does anonymity help us understand this Tradition? How do we practice anonymity in terms of this Tradition?

7. Discuss any bridges between this Tradition and other Traditions. What do these bridges teach us about our group?

8. What more can we do to bring the principles of this Tradition into our group efforts? What could we do differently to better fulfill our primary purpose?

In Service

Tradition Ten keeps us focused on our primary purpose and away from those issues that might divert or distract us. We believe in recovery through total abstinence from mood- and mind-altering drugs, and our program is founded on the principle of one addict helping another. When we operate in unity and keep our focus where it belongs, this seems natural and obvious. When we get involved in issues beyond our primary purpose, our attention is almost immediately diverted away from the newcomer.

Tradition Ten simplifies a whole range of issues for us. Learning the basics about working with the public *before* we try to do PR or H&I work is important. It gives us a foundation in principle and a set of answers to difficult questions that keep us from being drawn into controversy. We read, discuss, practice, and don't go alone. When we are able to explain clearly and simply what NA can and cannot provide, it is easier to stay out of controversy.

The easiest way to honor Tradition Ten is to keep it simple. There is so much that isn't any of our business. We can spend valuable time speculating about what NA's positions on particular outside issues would be, if we had them. We do much better when we focus on inside issues: What is our message, and how best do we carry it? If we take a position on anything other than our own message, we risk alienating those who need our help. Outside issues divert us; when we lose our focus, disunity and discord rush in. Insulating ourselves from public controversy and inviting a loving Power into our decisions foster an atmosphere of unity, goodwill, and recovery.

We consider our audience. When we share in a recovery meeting, we may be asking for help as much as carrying a message. When we share in an institutional setting, we focus more on the message and less on ourselves: We share how NA works for us. In a PR setting, our goal is not to make the same kind of empathetic connection we do in a regular meeting or in H&I; we share what NA is and is not, and its role in the community. Contesting the opinions of others or arguing the relative merits of different approaches draws us into controversy. With practice, we sidestep those questions and redirect the discussion to something we *can* talk about: Narcotics Anonymous.

We don't want to be so extreme that we act as if any engagement with another organization is affiliation, or that any involvement with the outside world is drawing us into controversy. We cooperate with other organizations so that addicts have a chance to hear our message, and we participate in the world because we are a part of it. We participate with a clear understanding of our purpose and the limits of what we can say or do. There are times when we are seen to represent the Fellowship even when we do not intend to. Traditions Ten and Eleven work together to help us draw and maintain that line. We pay attention to the difference between our own positions and those of Narcotics Anonymous. NA can feel like so much a part of us that we forget where we begin and NA ends. Indeed, some of us will say that NA is a part of every aspect of our lives; still, there are times when we speak for the Fellowship and times when we do not.

One of the most insidious ways we get distracted is that servants become more important than the service. Our diversions—allowing ourselves to be distracted or drawn into controversy—often begin with a sense of self-importance. We may get diverted in this way when we don't feel heard or respected. Sometimes the most powerful way we carry our message is to listen—to our Higher Power and to each other. A loving Higher Power works most powerfully through us when we can let go of the need to hear our own voice and strive to hear the conscience of the group instead. When anonymity guides our service efforts, we can let go of the need to be right, to be recognized, or to accumulate power.

Sometimes outside issues begin to feel like inside issues, and we can be drawn into controversy and disunity because conflicts from the outside world creep into meetings, or because policies and practices of other organizations have an impact on NA. Time, thought, prayer, and patience help us find principled responses. We can have a hard time leaving a question open. If we give too much attention or energy to a question, it begins to feel like a crisis. Distinguishing between anxiety and emergency takes practice and objectivity. When outside issues seem to affect the atmosphere of recovery or the quality of our meetings, we are often more successful when we look for ways to strengthen the atmosphere from within, rather than trying to control things outside of NA. Service meetings and workshops can be vital places for discussion, brainstorming, sharing experience, and offering support to groups struggling with issues that affect our ability to carry the message. Just as in our personal recovery, we don't have to do it alone. We don't have many new problems in service; many of our struggles have been addressed in some form or another before, somewhere in NA. Most of our problems have more than one potential solution, as well. When we ask for experience, strength, and hope, and listen with an open mind, we discover solutions we hadn't imagined.

WORKSHOP QUESTIONS

The questions below offer a way to begin—or continue—a service discussion or workshop focused on this Tradition.

1. When asked for NA's opinion on outside issues, how do we respond? How might we use such an inquiry as an opportunity to build positive public relations?

2. What are some specific ways our service body has been drawn into controversy? Can any of those situations be turned into PR opportunities?

3. When do we seem most vulnerable to being drawn into controversy? What tools do we have to prepare for these situations before they arise?

4. What role does this service body have in helping groups face challenges related to outside issues? What can we do to support groups that are facing such challenges?

5. Are there any outside issues currently affecting NA in any of our communities? What are those issues, and how can we address them without taking a stance or forming an opinion on anything other than our message?

6. How might an awareness of current or local outside issues help us in our efforts to carry the message? How can we seek to understand and respond to outside issues that affect how we carry the message, without being drawn into controversy?

7. How does this Tradition help us understand anonymity? How does anonymity help us understand this Tradition? How do we practice anonymity in terms of this Tradition?

8. Discuss any bridges between this Tradition and one or more of the Twelve Concepts. What do these bridges teach us about our service efforts?

9. What more can we do to bring the principles of this Tradition into our service efforts? What could we do differently to better carry out our services?

NA has a single purpose, a single promise, and a simple message. Just as trees gain strength from deep, steady roots, our Fellowship draws strength from the simple message of recovery at the root of all we do. By remaining true to our message, we are able to weather any storm. Our spiritual foundation supports us, and our Higher Power sustains us.

When we work the Steps, recovery is evident even if we don't speak a word. We turn away from public opinion and focus on our work. We are clear enough on our motives and purpose that we can resist being drawn into public controversy. Over and over, we see members from rival nations or neighborhoods, from different faiths or families, come to love and trust each other in the rooms of NA. We recover together in a spirit of unity. We protect that unity by refusing even the most tempting, noble, obvious, or awful invitations to engage in controversy. Because NA has no opinion on outside issues, each of us is free to think for ourselves as we recover.

*Our public relations policy is based
on attraction rather than promotion.
We need always maintain personal anonymity
at the level of press, radio, and films.*

TRADITION

It's difficult to describe recovery, and for many of us, the pain of active addiction can be just as hard to put into words. It's not just that we come in with secrets. We don't have language for our experience. Chapter Eight in our Basic Text describes "the wordless language of empathy" that connects us to each other and brings us hope.

When we find the message in our experience, what we have been through becomes useful. Our message is powerful because it is true. We listen to each other like our lives depend on it. When we hear another addict get to the exact nature of their experience, honestly and clearly, it changes us. The details don't matter. We connect with another addict's message because the truth is not just something we hear; it's something we feel. And when another addict helps us make sense of our experience by sharing their own, we begin to recover.

In our relations with the public, as in our recovery meetings, we simply tell the truth about the NA program and how it works for us. Personal anonymity frees us from ourselves; we can hear the message, and carry the message, free from the need to protect or prove anything.

Practicing personal anonymity is essential in a program of attraction. Anonymity takes us beyond what we believe about ourselves or each other. Empathy brings us to the truth, and we share it in language beyond words.

Tradition Eleven

Tradition Eleven tells us about our public relations policy. We engage with the world outside our meetings so that addicts can find us. We use the term *public relations* because we build and maintain ongoing relationships with people and organizations outside NA in order to reach addicts seeking recovery. Our goal in public relations work is always the same: We want addicts to come to a meeting and experience Narcotics Anonymous. Nothing we can say in a presentation, on a bus poster, or even in our literature can substitute for the identification we experience in the atmosphere of recovery found in an NA meeting. Hearing addicts share their experience, seeing recovery in action, feeling the love in the room—all this is as much a part of the process as the work we do on the Steps.

There are no promises we could make, no comparisons or endorsements, no claims or opinions that could be as powerful as experience, strength, and hope. Sharing from the heart is the most attractive thing we have to offer. Helping addicts find us, explaining NA to those around us, ensuring that it's safe for addicts to attend meetings—these are goals of our public relations policy. Our message—that any addict can stop using drugs, lose the desire to use, and find a new way to live—is all we have to give, and it is sufficient to change the lives of addicts all over the world.

Ultimately, Tradition Eleven is about the practice of goodwill inside and outside Narcotics Anonymous. Like so many things in recovery, how we do the work is as important as the work we do. A public relations policy based on attraction requires us to practice self-control: We cannot let enthusiasm run away with us, either by making promises or promotional claims about the program or by presenting ourselves as representatives of our anonymous Fellowship. It's not appropriate for members to be associated with the NA name in any form of media that is available to the general public. The *PR Handbook* and *PR Basics* booklet include discussion of our principles along with practical suggestions to help us work with the public. The guidance offered in those resources and the wisdom of our experienced trusted servants can help us practice PR more effectively. To carry out our policy of "attraction, rather than promotion," we present ourselves and our program with humility, honesty, and simplicity, and we allow the miracle of recovery to speak for itself.

For us, attraction means simply sharing how NA works, and that it works. The power of our message is in our honesty. Promotion would be to make guarantees or promises, set an individual member up as a "model recovering addict," or suggest that NA is the best or only way to recover. If we are not careful, our passion for NA could lead us to compromise the anonymity of ourselves or others, disrupt local services, and mislead others about NA. When we trust NA to be attractive to those seeking recovery, we can avoid the impulse to promote our program of recovery, and the challenges that would result from doing so.

Basing our policy on attraction means we must pay attention to what is attractive—the NA message. We work to create a space where addicts feel safe and comfortable and the message is clear. Unity, hospitality, and empathy serve to create an atmosphere in which addicts can recover. When there are members in the room with days and with decades; when there is diversity of experience and culture; when we are open to new people and welcoming to one another, we are attractive. Each of us is responsible for making a meeting attractive.

Our recovery is real, and so is our concern for the addict who still suffers. Our numbers are impressive, but our lives are even more so; the reality of Narcotics Anonymous speaks more powerfully than statistics or slogans. Around the world, addicts are recovering in Narcotics Anonymous. Each time an addict gets to experience the message in a way she or he can understand, we all grow. When a local translations committee completed translation of the Basic Text, one of the members smiled and said, "Now no one has the excuse that we don't have literature in our language!" Our principles are universal. They work for addicts in all walks of life, in scores of languages, with all kinds of religious and cultural beliefs. The growth of NA is proof of the power of our message. Still, even if we have millions of members, if we don't welcome the addict who walks through the door today, we are not attractive.

The personal anonymity this Tradition demands also offers protection. It protects us from the notoriety that might threaten our own recovery, it protects the program from our personal shortcomings, and it sets the NA message free to do its work beyond the limits our personalities present. The spirit of recovery that comes through our meetings is greater than the sum of its parts; each of us matters, and each of us serves best when we bring our experience, strength, and hope in a spirit of anonymity, allowing it to become part of the greater whole.

WORD BY WORD

Define, expand on, or clarify the words or phrases from this Tradition, one at a time or in relation to each other, for writing or discussion with your sponsor or other NA members.

Example: level

The word *level*, in Tradition Eleven, refers to a position relative to other things. Tradition Eleven prompts us to set things in relation to each other, to find equivalences. Sometimes this is easy and obvious; at other times the challenge this presents is startling. Tradition Eleven was written before the internet existed and before even television was in wide distribution. We communicate much differently today, and the media by which we communicate continue to evolve. So when we see the phrase "at the level of press, radio, and films," we are obliged to ask: What is equivalent today? What is "at the level" that press, radio, and films were when our program began? We need to think about the spirit of the Tradition—the principle at its core—as we consider how to apply it now. What does it mean to maintain our personal anonymity in a much less private world? We are called to practice this Tradition with more vigilance than ever.

SPIRITUAL PRINCIPLES

Each Tradition embodies a variety of spiritual principles. The list of principles and values below may be useful as we consider applications of this Tradition. Explore them in writing or discussion with your sponsor or other NA members. If other principles or values not listed below seem relevant for you, include those as well.

- faith
- fidelity
- humility
- unity

- service
- prudence
- respect
- wisdom

- anonymity
- discernment
- goodwill

- integrity
- accountability
- gratitude

Example: respect

Respect is a particularly challenging principle for many of us. Practicing this principle doesn't necessarily mean that others respect us; it means we offer others the respect we wish for ourselves, and that we respect ourselves enough to walk in dignity and quiet strength. We don't fight for respect; we demonstrate it. We earn the respect of others by being respectful and respectable ourselves, by standing on the merits of our program, and by resisting the impulse to boast or brag, to defend or argue. We can explain who and what we are with clarity, simplicity, and serenity. We no longer need to sacrifice our self-respect for approval. Our actions and demeanor show our respect for ourselves and our program. Anonymity is a key principle in our practice of respect: We each set aside our desire for recognition or approval—or our desire to hide—and stand together in dignity.

For Members

Tradition Eleven asks us to consider our personal anonymity and NA's relations with the public at the same time. Tradition Eleven asks us to practice restraint. We do not call attention to ourselves personally, even when we are sharing about the miracle of recovery in our lives. The practice of personal anonymity allows our recovery to speak for itself and allows us to live free of the risk that would come with being a spokesperson for NA. Tradition Eleven tells us that not only is the truth enough—any attempt at promotion thins out the truth, takes away from its power.

Tradition Eleven speaks about *personal* anonymity, keeping our membership in NA confidential, where Tradition Twelve discusses anonymity as the principle at the foundation of all our Traditions. Respecting our own anonymity and that of our fellows is a great responsibility. In early recovery, we may not be concerned about whether people outside NA know we are addicts. Once our anonymity is compromised, we can't get it back. Once our families or employers know, they know. For some of us, personal anonymity is vital. A casual mention could put our occupation or family status at risk. If we make that choice for someone else, we rob them of the opportunity to decide for themselves.

When people know we are in NA, we represent NA whether we mean to or not. Tradition Eleven tells us that the choice to reveal our membership comes with an obligation to protect NA's public reputation. Even if we insist that we don't intend to represent NA, to the public we often do. A member explained, "Every time I take a meeting into the county jail, I represent NA to both the inmates and their jailors. Every time I wear an NA T-shirt, I need to be aware that my actions—good or bad, in person or online—reflect on our program in action to anyone watching. I need to act right when my actions can affect someone's opinion about NA." Using social media puts us "in public" more than we tend to think about. The old saying is true: We may be the only Basic Text someone ever reads. Each of us is engaging in public relations every time we are in public. Our behavior in a restaurant after a meeting carries a message to everyone there. When we wear NA T-shirts or jewelry, talk loudly about our recovery or our addiction—people notice. The knowledge that "we are PR" is one more reason we try to practice principles in all our affairs.

People are attracted to NA when they see the program work in our lives. We don't pretend that recovery gives us a perfect or conflict-free life; often, the fact that we struggle and get through it clean is what makes recovery attractive. "My sister dragged me to meetings and that never worked," one member recalled. "But over the years, I saw her life change and I knew NA was working. When I was ready, her example was powerful." If an addict doesn't want to get clean, we can't help. When we refrain from pushing our way on others, they are more likely to come to us when they do want help. We don't make false promises or guarantees, but we do make ourselves available so that when an addict is ready, they can find us.

When we try to practice anonymity with an inflated ego, it hurts. That pain shows that we have room for growth. Anonymity requires ego deflation. Practicing namelessness leads us to deeper understandings of selflessness. We experiment with anonymity: doing good deeds that no one knows about; doing service that no one sees; keeping the confidences of others. We start to experience the gift of giving freely. We begin to feel integrity, to know who we are without depending on others to tell us. Much of what has been written in NA about anonymity frames it as a sacrifice. In reality, it's a gift. It's freedom.

When we don't respect our own anonymity, the spiritual damage can make us sick. We have a hard time being vulnerable, asking for help, or trusting others with confidences we haven't kept ourselves. When we set ourselves up as an authority about NA or in NA, we set ourselves apart— which ultimately means we end up alone. We give ourselves permission to be human, and we free ourselves from the need to be right all the time. No one of us speaks for NA.

Technology, communication, and the world at large have changed dramatically since the Eleventh Tradition first took shape. Our relationship to technology is much more intimate than it once was. It can be hard to tell the difference between our public and private lives. A great deal of our online activity is public, and we don't always have control over the flow of information. As members of NA, applying Tradition Eleven means we have a responsibility to think about how we maintain our anonymity online. As a Fellowship, we must consider the challenges presented to anonymity, and as members, we must find practices of anonymity that honor the needs of NA. Understanding spiritual principles allows us to make wise decisions. We don't all agree on which types of online interactions require anonymity and which don't, but it merits serious consideration from each of us.

Our service pamphlet *Social Media and Our Guiding Principles* is a resource for practicing Tradition Eleven. We see from a new perspective when we consider the effects of our actions. For some of us, participating in social media is an important part of our lives; others don't make use of these sites at all. Our ability to control our social media presence is limited in part by the actions and awareness—or lack of awareness—of those around us. Our anonymity is more often compromised through thoughtlessness than malice. Addressing these mishaps can be an opportunity to build understanding, or it can leave us feeling alone and attacked. Raising our concerns, and responding to the concerns of others in a spirit of love and unity, allows us to come to an understanding we can live with. Over and over, Tradition Eleven teaches us about the practical application of humility and goodwill.

The most important things we do in Narcotics Anonymous come from a spirit of selflessness. Setting our needs aside in service to a greater good is an antidote for the self-obsession that plagues us. When we accept ourselves as we are, owning our assets and liabilities, we are more attractive than when we pretend to be something we're not. Similarly, the NA public relations policy depends on us staying true to exactly who we are and what we do, rather than making outrageous claims. Tradition Eleven speaks to the value of attraction, rather than promotion. As human beings, and as a Fellowship, we are enough.

QUESTIONS FOR MEMBERS

The questions below offer a way to begin—or continue—the process of writing, reflection, and discussion of this Tradition with your sponsor or other NA members.

IN NA

1. What role did attraction or promotion play in how I found NA? How does this shape my actions or attitudes as a member?

2. Under what circumstances might the public view me as a representative of NA? Does my anonymity need protection in relationships with the public that do not involve press, radio, or films?

3. How do I recognize when it's important or necessary to maintain my anonymity? How do I maintain personal anonymity at the level of press, radio, film, and other public media?

4. Under what circumstances do I protect my anonymity? Under what circumstances am I open about my membership in NA? How do I decide what's right for me and for NA?

5. Do I ever want to share about addiction or recovery in public? Have there been times when I have tried to promote NA on a public level? How can I talk about addiction or recovery while maintaining my personal anonymity?

6. When have I compromised someone else's anonymity? When has my anonymity been compromised, and what were the consequences? What could we have done differently? How can I respond in situations where that's a possibility?

7. How does our relationship to anonymity change after death? Do our departed members still merit personal anonymity? How do we honor them without compromising that principle for them or for NA?

8. How does this Tradition help me understand anonymity? How does anonymity help me understand this Tradition? How do I practice anonymity in terms of this Tradition?

9. Describe any bridges between this Tradition and one or more of the Twelve Steps. What do these bridges teach me about my recovery?

10. What more can I do to put the principles of this Tradition into action? How would applying this Tradition change my attitudes and actions?

IN ALL OUR AFFAIRS

11. How have I applied this Tradition outside NA? How else might the principles of this Tradition guide my thinking or my actions?

12. In my day-to-day life, how can I serve as an attractive example of NA recovery? In what ways might my actions be unattractive?

13. Under what circumstances would I reveal my NA membership? What are some differences in the way I practice anonymity with family, friends, and coworkers, at school, and elsewhere?

14. Are there any friends or family members to whom I've wanted or tried to promote NA? What were the results? What is the difference between attraction and promotion in those situations?

15. What does the phrase "responsible, productive member of society" mean to me? How do I view my personal reputation?

16. Are there other areas of my life in which anonymity might be important? How do I maintain my anonymity in those situations?

17. Do I need to practice attraction or promotion with any other clubs or organizations I'm involved with? Does the practice of Tradition Eleven in NA teach me anything that could be useful in understanding membership in other groups?

18. Does maintaining my personal anonymity ever make it feel like I'm living a double life? Am I sometimes overly public about my membership in NA? How do I maintain personal anonymity and personal integrity at the same time?

For Groups

Groups are the face of NA as much as they are its heart. For the most part, groups are not engaged in the kind of public relations work that service bodies undertake, but interacting with an NA group is often the first or only experience members of the public have with NA. Our group's relationships—with the facility in which we meet, the neighbors around the meeting, and the businesses we frequent—all reflect on NA as a whole. Any time we interact with the world beyond our meetings, we are PR.

Simple things—being clear on our group's conscience, knowing how to contact the facility and having designated group members who interact with them, being consistent and on time with our payment, and leaving the space better than we found it—build relationships that last. When we are responsible and consistent, we build trust. The trust we build in the community makes people more comfortable with NA, makes it easier for us to find meeting space, and helps us gain access to addicts in hospitals and institutions. Our practice of goodwill helps the Fellowship to grow.

When we are approached with questions, it's good to be prepared. If we are clear as a group and as members about what NA is, what we do and what we don't do, our explanation can be simple and clear. When we are well versed in our Traditions, we make it easier for others to respect our Traditions, and to respect us. When our group meets the curiosity of its neighbors with a friendly curiosity about the world around us, our communications can be more than one-way information delivery. We are always seeking ways to reach the addicts around us, and as we inform others about what NA is we also find out more about how we can reach out. Most of all, when we foster goodwill with those around us, we make NA attractive and secure as a part of the community.

In our groups, Tradition Eleven has more to do with how we carry the message than about our relationship to other organizations or "at the level of press, radio and films." In our group we create an atmosphere of attraction; we remind one another to practice personal anonymity as well as keeping confidences; and we strive to welcome and inform anyone who is new or observing what NA is about.

We don't tell people how to share, but we create an atmosphere of recovery, a group format, and a group conscience that makes room for all to feel welcome, share honestly, and find hope in Narcotics Anonymous. A safe, secure atmosphere of recovery is attractive. We all are responsible to ensure that addicts feel welcome and have the opportunity to experience Narcotics Anonymous. Before we got clean, many of us were accustomed to seeing others as a means to get something. It can take some of us a while to regard each other with respect and care; in our groups we come to understand one another's humanity. When a group ensures that a newcomer is approached by members who are trustworthy and concerned, we protect the addict and the Fellowship.

Carrying the message is an act of faith and courage. There is a balance between not promoting NA (or ourselves) and carrying a message of hope. We allow our experience to speak for itself, and trust that others will hear what they need. We don't sell recovery like a used car. Our job in carrying the message is not to present a sales pitch, but to share experience, strength, and hope. We make NA available to all addicts. We cannot force recovery on anyone, no matter how badly we want recovery for them, and we don't need to make false promises or guarantees to be attractive—our message of hope is strong and true. We don't need to promote NA in order to share a powerful message. We share our experience and trust others to find what they need.

GROUP INVENTORY QUESTIONS _____

The questions below offer ways to begin—or continue—group inventory or discussion focused on this Tradition.

1. What can our group do to help make our meetings attractive, safe, and welcoming?

2. Does our group have a strong home group identity? Do we celebrate group anniversaries, have home group T-shirts, or have other group-specific events or customs? How do we enjoy these in a way that is based on attraction, not promotion?

3. What in our meeting could be seen as promoting NA or a particular group, rather than seeking to make NA attractive?

4. How does our group work to make sure we are viewed in a positive light by the facility where we meet? In the neighborhood where our meetings are held?

5. Does our group use any form of social media for communication between members? If so, how can we preserve members' anonymity when we do? How can we take care not to exclude members who don't use social media?

6. How should our group respond if we are asked by the local media to answer questions about drug addiction, about recovery, or other topics?

7. How does this Tradition help us understand anonymity? How does anonymity help us understand this Tradition? How do we practice anonymity in terms of this Tradition?

8. Discuss any bridges between this Tradition and other Traditions. What do these bridges teach us about our group?

9. What more can we do to bring the principles of this Tradition into our group efforts? What could we do differently to better fulfill our primary purpose?

In Service

We let people know who we are, what we do, and where to find us. Tradition Eleven provides our service bodies with essential guidance. First, we don't make bold claims about our program of recovery, and don't attempt to push it on anyone; and second, we must be careful in how we present ourselves as members of NA when we interact with members of the public.

Public relations and fellowship development go hand in hand. Fellowship development helps support the growth and stability of NA communities, and PR helps to build ongoing relationships with the people and institutions that help NA to be recognized and welcomed by the communities, institutions, and governments that may support or prevent our growth. We build relationships over time in which these entities can learn about NA—and in which we can learn how we can better communicate what we do.

Although the Eleventh Tradition is simple and straightforward, we have needed a wide range of service material over the course of our history to guide our trusted servants on interactions with the public. "Recovery and Relapse" in our Basic Text reminds us, "Relationships can be a terribly painful area for us," and our difficulties in relating to others do not end with our personal relationships. In NA service, relationships with the public affect our ability to carry the message. Taking Tradition Eleven to heart as we serve is how we ensure that those relationships have positive results.

Developing a public relations policy is more than just reaching out based on our whims. Discussion, planning, and being strategic about how we carry out and sustain that policy is important. Random or inconsistent outreach can do more harm to our reputation than not reaching out at all; PR is one of the areas of service in which we must be most cautious. It can also be some of the most vital, and rewarding, work we do in Narcotics Anonymous. When our public relations efforts are successful, we see it not only in the numbers of newcomers finding their way to NA but in the goodwill we encounter in the community. It gets easier to find meeting space; institutions welcome our presence; professionals are more willing to refer addicts to NA and to listen to us at events and conferences. Ultimately our goal is always the same: to allow more addicts to stop using drugs and find a new way to live. We don't have to promise or compromise to build those relationships: we do have to pay attention to the communities in which we meet and the concerns of those we reach out to.

Continuity can be so important in these relationships. We don't have to send the same people every time we reach out, but others should know how to reach us, and that if they contact us they will receive a prompt and constructive reply. Just as we want to be available when the addict is ready, we want to ensure that when others want to learn about Narcotics Anonymous, we are ready to rise to the opportunity. In some regions, outreach efforts in parks, at health fairs, or even at festivals have become routine; in others, relationships with correctional facilities are so strong that NA members behind the walls are able to participate in NA events on the outside—either virtually or in person.

We carry the NA message and work to ensure that addicts seeking recovery will know where to find us. That life-saving message may be all an addict needs to have a chance. Our service efforts include a wider audience than our Twelfth Step or our meetings. Helping the different types of people we interact with to see the attractiveness of our message and our program requires thought and creativity. Our *Public Relations Handbook* offers some of our collective experience with how our service efforts can be most effective in helping addicts seeking recovery to find NA.

Some communities have experienced public relations efforts that were so successful that they overwhelmed the local groups. "We scheduled some presentations with local government officials, including some drug court counselors," one PR chair shared. "They loved us so much that our meetings were suddenly full. The people chairing meetings had a hard time keeping the meetings running smoothly, and one group even received a noise complaint." In order to be successful, service efforts need not only to attract more people to our meetings, but also to coordinate with groups to ensure that the groups can support and sustain the growth.

We create events and activities to build unity, celebrate together, have fun, and sometimes to raise funds. While the main focus of this type of service isn't to engage in public relations, the events we hold are still very much a part of NA's public image. Our events and activities often bring trusted servants—and other members—into contact with the public. Whether it's the business where we print our T-shirts or the hotel lobby where our members proudly wear those T-shirts, when we interact with the public as NA members, we must be mindful of our behavior. One member shared, "At our big convention every year, I'm always thinking of how the hotel workers and convention center staff see us. If we are examples of NA recovery, maybe a worker will think of NA when they have a friend or family member who needs help with a drug problem." No matter what the circumstances, when we're in situations where the public sees us as NA members, our actions can make a difference in an addict's life.

Our trusted servants have a responsibility to treat everyone with dignity and respect. Similarly, we all have an obligation to treat our trusted servants well. We are sometimes prone to an "us and them" mentality, and one place in NA where we see this often is at events when there is a feeling of division between the trusted servants and the members attending. The Second Tradition essay in, *It Works: How and Why* reminds us that "leadership in NA is a service, not a class of membership." We treat each other as fellows, whether we're the chair of a convention committee feeling a great sense of responsibility for the event, or a member attending a campout with lots of ideas about how the committee could do a better job. When we treat each other well regardless of our role or position, both our recovery program and our service efforts benefit.

We have a commitment to personal anonymity at the level of press, radio, and film. Though this Tradition was written in a time before television was common or the internet existed, the guidance applies just as well to those forms of public media as any other. The Narcotics Anonymous name should not be associated with any individual member, as a member, in any form of media that is available to the general public. Whether a journalist calls to interview an addict, or a committee decides to use the internet as a place to hold service discussions, we take care not to put any of our members on public view as members of NA. This may mean setting careful terms for how a conversation can happen, or devoting time and effort to ensure that the online tools we use to communicate about NA service aren't visible to the general public.

Trusted servants are not obligated to maintain personal anonymity in every interaction with those outside NA. As an example, trusted servants often must disclose their names and other personal information in order to rent space for a meeting or an event. When the press or media are involved, however, protection of the NA name means that members do not have the ability to break their own anonymity as members of NA. Some NA members do choose to identify as recovering addicts in the media; as long as the NA name is not mentioned or implied, discussing addiction can be a personal choice. We may choose to admit to being an addict, but Tradition Eleven instructs us to keep our NA membership out of public media.

Tradition Eleven mentions a public relations *policy*. In NA service, we have plenty of resources—handbooks, guidelines, and more. These tools all help us to serve well, but ultimately the spirit of the Eleventh Tradition is our best guide. We serve most effectively when our service helps NA to be attractive to all who may need it.

WORKSHOP QUESTIONS

The questions below offer a way to begin—or continue—a service discussion or workshop focused on this Tradition.

1. What is the difference between attraction and promotion? How does this difference influence the services we carry out?

2. How does the behavior of our members around our meetings or in our service efforts reflect on NA as a whole? Are we serving as examples of recovery in our community, or do our relations with our neighbors reflect poorly on NA?

3. What is the role of public relations service in the growth of NA in our community?

4. What tools do we have to assess the PR needs in our community? Are there professionals in our community who may not know about NA? What do we do to make sure that professionals are able to find NA in order to send addicts to us?

5. Are our PR efforts planned and considered, or do they happen intermittently when someone gets interested? How consistently do we follow through?

6. What holds us back from doing PR? Are our reservations based in planning or fear? How can we support each other in our PR efforts? How can we help our groups to carry the message when our PR efforts are successful?

7. How does our policy of attraction rather than promotion affect the service we do beyond PR? How else might this guide our efforts? Is there anything our service body is doing now that might be improved or changed by considering this policy?

8. Why shouldn't any single member be a spokesperson for NA? What can we do to avoid situations where a member might be seen as a spokesperson for us?

9. What are some challenges or opportunities social media presents to our public relations efforts? How do we ensure that the guidance of this Tradition is applied to our use of communication tools? How do we protect personal anonymity and NA's reputation on the internet or in social media? What can we do to restore NA's reputation once it's been compromised?

10. How does this Tradition help us understand anonymity? How does anonymity help us understand this Tradition? How do we practice anonymity in terms of this Tradition?

11. Discuss any bridges between this Tradition and one or more of the Twelve Concepts. What do these bridges teach us about our service efforts?

12. What more can we do to bring the principles of this Tradition into our service efforts? What could we do differently to better carry out our services?

Our Traditions help us to see how NA fits in the world. Traditions Six and Seven clarify that we do not align with or indebt ourselves to anyone outside of NA. Traditions Ten and Eleven provide us with a specific vision for what NA says to the public: We express no opinion on issues other than NA, and when we speak about our program of recovery, we simply describe how it has worked for us. Our Third Tradition reminds us that recovery works best when members are free to come and go as they please, and our Eleventh Tradition frees us from the need to push our program on others. Navigating the relationship between NA and the outside world is challenging. Our service materials, recovery literature, and experienced members help to guide us.

Each of us discovers our own motivations, on our own time, to humbly reach out for help from those who have found relief from addiction. As we listen to experience and suggestions and work the Steps, our lives improve. In turn, others will see the change in us and, as they are ready, seek out our experience, strength, and hope. The NA message does not need to be promoted. The fact that our program continues to prove itself in the lives of many addicts is attractive in itself.

*Anonymity is the spiritual foundation of
all our Traditions, ever reminding us to place
principles before personalities.*

TRADITION

12

When we share from the heart, we connect at the heart. Whether it's the first time or the thousandth, hearing an addict tell the truth has the power to crack us wide open if we set aside our judgment long enough to listen. Many of us have shared or heard someone share about the beauty of attending a meeting out of town: "The message was so clear, because I didn't know everyone's story."

Anonymity allows us to experience equality. We have spent so much of our lives measuring our own value against our beliefs about the value of others. Equality, acceptance, and welcome are a tremendous relief. Simply belonging can be refreshing.

We find a wellspring of hope in the lives of addicts recovering around us. When we let go of our own opinions, histories, and judgments of ourselves and each other, we can feel the presence of a Power in our meetings, and we can hear wisdom from any addict, if we are willing to listen for it. One member suggested that *any* is short for *anonymous*.

Anonymity opens us to grace. It frees us from obsession with self and society, and it allows us to recognize our Higher Power in the eyes of another human being. Anonymity allows us to rise above who we think we are.

We all have the ability to find knowledge of our Higher Power's will for us and the power to carry that out. Anonymity allows us to see it in ourselves and in another addict—any addict.

Tradition Twelve

Tradition Twelve guides us to let go of all that keeps us from unity. We set aside all the things that separate us and come together as "we." That *we* stands before everything we do. There is a vital link between Tradition Twelve and Tradition One; they frame our Traditions and establish the spirit in which our work will be done. When we embrace our anonymity, we recognize that our common welfare is also our personal welfare. We can see ourselves as part of the greater whole, and understand where we fit. Coming from the alienation of addiction into membership, into anonymity, frees us from the masks and pretenses that once got us through life. In anonymity we are finally allowed to be ourselves.

Our principles have a purpose, as we have a purpose. We don't recover by sitting around pondering mysteries; applying these principles creates a way of life, and a way to carry the message. This is a program of action, and our principles only work when we are using them. They gain meaning as we apply them. Tradition Twelve is not mysterious, but it grows in meaning and richness as we practice all our Traditions, pray and meditate, and discover the gifts within it. Until we incorporate a spiritual principle into our lives, it's a word on a page. We can only understand so much from reading a book—we must live it to understand.

For most of us, anonymity begins as letting go. We set aside our prejudices and beliefs about each other to place principles before each other's personalities, in order to hear the message. Soon we learn that it's not just other people's personalities we set aside; it's our own. We cannot fully practice the Traditions without working the Steps, and Tradition Twelve drives us to the work. Setting principles before personalities means, first, that we must understand principles, and second, that we must be able to recognize and set aside the chatter in our heads about who we are, and who others are, that keeps us from hearing. When we learn to listen, we open ourselves to the possibility of empathy.

What anonymity gives us is far greater than what it asks from us, although we may struggle sometimes with the surrender. Anonymity allows us to be human, and humane. When we are not defined by our success or failure we can let ourselves, and each other, off the hook. The anonymity Tradition Twelve describes supports and explains our personal anonymity, but it's bigger than that. Our spiritual foundation is not a question of whether we know each other's last names; it's that we accept each other regardless of who we are and what we have done. Anonymity is the beginning of equality; we allow each other to be members, to recover in dignity, and to carry the message to the best of our ability. The Twelve Traditions describe a Fellowship that takes its collective guidance from spiritual principles rather than from individual personalities. That selflessness is what the Twelfth Tradition means by the word *anonymity*, and it is the spiritual foundation on which NA is built.

 ## WORD BY WORD

Define, expand on, or clarify the words or phrases from this Tradition, one at a time or in relation to each other, for writing or discussion with your sponsor or other NA members.

Example: foundation

A *foundation* is a base on which something is built. The foundation stands under a structure, securing it and providing a steady footing. Our spiritual foundation grounds us and keeps us secure. It goes deep, and provides stability for everything we do. All of our efforts begin with unity and stand on a foundation of anonymity. When we work toward the greater good, allowing a loving Higher Power to be in charge, there is no limit to what we can build.

When the word *foundation* is used regarding a principle, it means that this idea is at the heart of everything that follows from it. Tradition Twelve says that anonymity is our spiritual foundation, which means that every other principle is built upon and supported by our application of anonymity.

SPIRITUAL PRINCIPLES

Each Tradition embodies a variety of spiritual principles. The list of principles and values below may be useful as we consider applications of this Tradition. Explore them in writing or discussion with your sponsor or other NA members. If other principles or values not listed below seem relevant for you, include those as well.

- faith
- fidelity
- humility
- unity

- service
- prudence
- respect
- wisdom

- anonymity
- discernment
- goodwill

- integrity
- accountability
- gratitude

Example: anonymity

Just as white light contains every other color within it, the principle of anonymity contains every other spiritual principle. The core of our disease is self-centeredness; its opposite is freedom from self. Anonymity is so much more than not being identified by name, or having no name; it means we let go of the things with which we have identified ourselves, and the ways in which we expect recognition. Only when we let go of our preconceived ideas of who we should be, or how we think we are perceived, do we get to find out who we are.

Anonymity means that we surrender to being part of something greater than ourselves. We are responsible to do the work to embrace our membership; when we allow ourselves that privilege, we never have to do it alone again. Anonymity frees us to be better than we have ever been. We don't have to worry about who we are and where we fit; we can be one of many, doing our Higher Power's will to the best of our ability, in a spirit of unity and goodwill.

For Members

Allowing ourselves to experience anonymity is a great gift. We learn to trust and be trustworthy. We learn to give with no expectations—not even acknowledgment. The exercise of simple, anonymous service, like setting up chairs or sweeping the floor after a meeting, helps us to feel like a part of the group. Some of us take this further, trying to do something good daily that no one knows about, or being of anonymous service in our communities.

When we first come to NA, we might think anonymity is just not knowing each other's last names or what we do outside NA—or we just see it as the most difficult word to pronounce in our readings. Outside NA, most of us experience a world where some people are in positions of authority or privilege depending on their job, their education, or their role in society. We may even be one of those who enjoy such privileges, but there is no room for this kind of status in NA. Each of us is simply carrying and receiving the message. This is one way we practice anonymity, and it guides us to place our principles before our personalities.

We are equals here, regardless of our cleantime, service position, sponsorship, or any role we play in our lives outside. This doesn't mean we leave our personalities at the door; all personalities are welcome in NA. By taking the focus off our personal differences, anonymity allows addicts of all backgrounds and personality types to recover together in unity. And yet, this Tradition does not insist that we eliminate or ignore our differences. The Tradition Twelve essay in *It Works: How and Why* tells us, "We enjoy the color, the compassion, the initiative, the rough-and-tumble liveliness that arises from the diverse personalities of our members. In fact, our diversity is our strength." Anonymity allows us to come together in all our diversity to support fellow members and fulfill our primary purpose. "I was raised with a certain set of beliefs about people, and my experience seemed to confirm those beliefs. In recovery, I got to see people for who they are, not what they are," said a member.

Placing principles before personalities protects us from our own defects of character. While it may take time for us to work through and trust the process, as we grow in our recovery we learn that we don't have to make our personalities smaller; it's through our differences and difficulties with each other that we learn how to practice principles. When we hear a message from a member we have conflict with, or see recovery working in the life of someone we had no hope for, we start to understand that open-mindedness doesn't just help us tolerate others. It broadens our ability to hope. When we see that the limits of our vision are not the limits of possibility, our faith blossoms. Learning to hear each other, in meetings and in service, takes practice. We test each other's limits all the time, and each of us has particular challenges with members or behaviors we cannot seem to tolerate. We don't have to like everyone in NA, but if we turn our attention to our reaction rather than the person or thing we're reacting to, we may find relief much sooner.

Anonymity provides us with safety, both in NA and in our spirit. When we let go of the need to judge and be judged, we can take risks, try new things or ideas, and continue to grow, secure in the love of the Fellowship. When we find ourselves outside that safety net, it's mostly because we choose not to be a part of. When we engage in selfish or destructive behaviors, we are separating ourselves—often long before we actually experience consequences. When we grasp or demand, we are not open to the selfless exchange that is happening around us. Pride can take us outside that circle. When arrogance and denial come together, we are in grave danger. We desperately want to be somebody important, but we are terrified that we are worthless. We forget about anonymity and go back into competition. The consequence is that again we feel isolated, alone, and separate. Coming back into the circle can take a great deal of courage, but once we make the leap it's not that hard. The love and acceptance we once found in the rooms is there waiting for us, if we are willing to accept it.

Anonymity is a two-way street. We need the safety anonymity gives us to grow and change, to take risks, and to keep coming back. But we also need to trust in the spirit of anonymity that the help we need will be available—even though it might not look like what, or who, we expected. There are some things we only learn through pain, and there are times in recovery when each of us will hurt. Humility helps us to practice anonymity; we can let go of our demands and expectations of others. Faith in the Fellowship of NA is not the same as relying on individuals. None of us is perfect, and none of us is perfectly patient or available. Being willing to accept the help we need regardless of where it comes from can be extraordinarily challenging. When we let go of our expectations, we can give where it's needed, receive where it's offered, and feel the presence of our Higher Power in the exchange.

Tradition Twelve brings calm to our lives. We can let go of drama and the need for attention, and see what is real. In our lives outside NA as well, letting go of the focus on personality—including our own—can allow us to see what is happening, what we need, and what we can do. Not every area of our lives is anonymous, but our practice of anonymity in Narcotics Anonymous, and our understanding of anonymity as a spiritual principle, grants us safety and security at our personal foundation. Living the principles of our Traditions teaches us that we have value, that our lives have meaning, and that we are worthy of love and acceptance.

QUESTIONS FOR MEMBERS

The questions below offer a way to begin—or continue—the process of writing, reflection, and discussion of this Tradition with your sponsor or other NA members.

IN NA

1. What are some differences between the personal anonymity in Tradition Eleven and the principle of anonymity as it's expressed in Tradition Twelve?

2. What are some ways that I put principles before personalities when I'm in a meeting? When I talk to my sponsor? When I sponsor other members? When I talk to newcomers? When I talk to other members?

3. How do I practice principles before personalities when I have strong feelings about someone, good or bad?

4. Does my desire to honor those who came before me sometimes affect how I practice the principle of anonymity? Do members who serve, or who have served, ever seem more important than others? Do I view NA members as fitting into any sort of hierarchy?

5. When do I struggle with the principle of anonymity? Are there times when equality is a struggle for me, or when that idea makes me uncomfortable? Do I ever want to "pull rank" or establish authority? Am I intimidated by some members, or are there times I just assume that they're right?

6. Do I respect the confidentiality of meetings? Is sharing what is heard in a meeting always wrong? How do I determine the difference between gossiping and expressing concern?

7. When do I struggle to serve selflessly? Do I want personal credit for successes, or feel that members should take personal blame for mistakes?

8. How can serving with humility give me the opportunity to know freedom from the bonds of self? When have I experienced this for myself?

9. Do members give up their anonymity when it comes to mistakes or failures in service, including theft or other types of inappropriate actions? How do we balance the need to hold one another accountable with the need to keep principles before personalities?

10. How can I express my gratitude or appreciation for another member, present or past, in the spirit of equality we value in NA? How do I honor the contributions of members in a way that respects the guidance of Tradition Twelve?

11. How does my practice of anonymity help to foster NA unity? How does NA unity help me place principles before personalities?

12. How do these Traditions help me understand anonymity? How does anonymity help me understand these Traditions? How do I practice anonymity in terms of the Traditions?

13. Describe any bridges between this Tradition and one or more of the Twelve Steps. What do these bridges teach me about my recovery?

14. What more can I do to put the principles of this Tradition into action? How would applying this Tradition change my attitudes and actions?

IN ALL OUR AFFAIRS

15. How have I applied this Tradition outside NA? How else might the principles of this Tradition guide my thinking or my actions?

16. What would it mean for anonymity to be my spiritual foundation? What does this principle bring to my life, or change about my thinking?

17. How does practicing principles before personalities help me to experience unity outside NA? Can I apply the principle of anonymity in my work, in my family, or in my community in ways that would foster unity?

18. What is at risk when I place personalities before principles in my personal relationships, at work, in school, or in community organizations? How and when do I need to place principles before personalities in these areas?

19. Do I struggle to accept credit for my accomplishments outside NA? How do I balance these principles in places where receiving credit or recognition is appropriate?

20. How can I apply principles of this Tradition in areas of my life outside of NA where not everyone is regarded as equal?

21. Are there times in my life outside NA when I want to "call someone out" in a way that would be hurtful or destructive? How can Tradition Twelve help me to navigate conflict or anger?

22. What other areas of my life would benefit from the application of selflessness? What would change in my relationships if I approached them from a spirit of anonymity?

23. How do humility, anonymity, and unity work together and separately in my life? What are some ways I practice these principles? When I come from a place of unity and anonymity, how does my experience of the world change?

For Groups

Tradition Twelve makes clear that the principle of anonymity is at the core of all we do. Anonymity is so important to what we do, in fact, that it makes up half our name, Narcotics Anonymous. For many of us, our understanding of anonymity begins with recognition that recovery is easier when we can seek help for our problem with some measure of privacy. Anonymity includes keeping the identities of our fellow members confidential, but it is much more than that. Anonymity establishes our right to equal membership in NA and makes our groups a place where addicts of many backgrounds and unique personalities come together to share recovery. The result is an atmosphere of recovery capable of giving addicts enough hope to stay clean.

We come together as one, but in recovery we are neither nameless nor faceless. Our distinct personalities, our diversity, and our experience are what make up Narcotics Anonymous. None of us is better or worse, more or less important, more or less worthy or likely to make it another day. Anonymity gives us all a break and gives us each a chance.

Recovery is not a measurable commodity. When we live the NA program to the best of our ability, we bring hope to the meeting. At some point in our recovery, each of us goes through some darkness. Facing challenges and struggling to live our principles doesn't take away the reality of our recovery. Our struggles are part of the process. Anonymity means that each of us brings what we have to the group, and from that material a message develops. Each of us is a part of that; none of us is the whole thing and none of us "ruins it," even when the best thing we're doing is not picking up.

Our practice of anonymity makes it possible for us to experience unity, and our contributions to the common welfare of NA improve our personal recovery. We are a Fellowship of talented, creative, dynamic, and resourceful people, but when we direct our energies only toward helping ourselves, many of us end up feeling isolated, alienated, and alone. When we turn our attention and our efforts toward helping each other, we may feel more like ourselves than we ever have. Recovery gives us the freedom not just to be ourselves but to see, perhaps for the first time, how valuable we truly are.

The anonymity we speak of in Tradition Twelve is much more than the ideas of namelessness or confidentiality many of us associate with the word *anonymous*. However, the practice of anonymity does involve being mindful of these concerns. Tradition Twelve in *It Works: How and Why* notes that many of our meeting formats include the statement that "what's said in this meeting stays in this meeting." We all benefit from the freedom that comes with being able to share from our hearts without being worried about public disclosure of what we said. It can also be helpful to keep in mind that no one practices all of our guiding principles perfectly at all times. We practice these principles to the best of our ability, just for today.

We value privacy and confidentiality in NA, but we also learn to practice discretion in what and how we share. The confidentiality we hope for in a meeting is not the same as the deep sanctity of the sponsorship relationship. We expect our sponsors to keep our confidences, and we build trust in others over time. Not everyone in a meeting will honor that same degree of confidentiality, even though we may wish they would. Strong groups foster an atmosphere where members can share freely, but anonymity is still not a guarantee of privacy. We each play a part in helping all our members feel safe and secure in sharing.

Anonymity is important at the group level for another reason: Our groups have their own identities. Our Fourth Tradition provides groups with the autonomy to conduct their meetings as they see fit, as long as they adhere to the guidance in the rest of the Traditions. The Fifth Tradition sets the job of carrying our message ahead of anything else a group does. The personality the group develops in its autonomy should always be in service to the task of carrying the message as best we can. This is one way in which groups place our principles first.

Another way can be found in the selection of trusted servants. The members who make up a home group typically lend their personalities to the identity of the group. Practicing the spirit of rotation when choosing our group trusted servants can go a long way in helping the group to develop an identity based on practices and principles rather than particular personalities.

The NA group, as *The Group Booklet* tells us, is "the foundation of the NA service structure." With anonymity as the spiritual foundation of all our Traditions, the NA groups can establish the spiritual tone for all of our NA service. Our groups are the place where our members first experience and learn what anonymity means in the context of our Fellowship. The better our groups embody the loving guidance found in all our Traditions, the better our members will be equipped to grow in recovery, serve selflessly, and contribute in the spirit of goodwill to our primary purpose.

GROUP INVENTORY QUESTIONS _____

The questions below offer ways to begin—or continue—group inventory or discussion focused on this Tradition.

1. What are some of the ways our group practices anonymity? How do these relate to how we treat each other and how we fulfill our primary purpose? How else is the spirit of anonymity practiced at our group?

2. How do we acknowledge the value of members' service contributions? How can we encourage selfless service while maintaining a focus on anonymity? Do we sometimes base our service on motives other than selflessness?

3. What can we do to help keep principles before personalities in our recovery meetings? In our group conscience/business meetings?

4. How do members' personalities contribute to our group's identity? Are there particular personalities that dominate or define us as a group or in our meetings? How do we keep principles first when our personalities are strong?

5. What processes do we go through to select our trusted servants? How does observing the principle of rotation help keep our group healthy?

6. Do we treat everyone who attends our meeting as equal? Are there some ways or times we fall short, and if so, how? What can we do to ensure that all members are shown respect?

7. What kinds of things are appropriate to take with us from the meeting, and what should we leave behind? What is the difference between anonymity and confidentiality? What responsibility do we have to help protect the confidentiality of those who share?

8. Are we more willing to tolerate bad behavior from some members than we are from others? Do we have different standards for use of time or other behavior within our meeting, depending on who's involved?

9. Might long-standing friendships or shared sponsorship within our group seem exclusive? How can our practice of unity extend to include everyone at the meeting? What draws our attention to the ways people might feel left out? What do we do when we notice?

10. How does this Tradition help us understand anonymity? How does anonymity help us understand this Tradition? How do we practice anonymity in terms of this Tradition?

11. Discuss any bridges between this Tradition and other Traditions. What do these bridges teach us about our group?

12. What more can we do to bring the principles of this Tradition into our group efforts? What could we do differently to better fulfill our primary purpose?

In Service

Being of service takes us out of ourselves and focuses us on the greater good. Service can be a tremendous relief—we get a reprieve from the self-centeredness at the core of our disease. It is a gift to be able to set aside the burden of self-obsession and focus on principles.

We have many reasons for getting involved in service, and sometimes those reasons are far from selfless. Most of us who have stuck around for years or decades have at some time or another found ourselves driven by mixed motives—to boost our egos or get recognition, or just to get our way. When we experience success or achieve big accomplishments in service, we may struggle to find comfort with selflessness once more. Even when we know better—we may not want our name over the door of the meeting hall, but we want the respect and credit that seem to be our due. No matter how justified we may feel, self-centered service can be destructive. If our work is not grounded in spiritual principles, at some level it may not be service. When we serve NA from a genuine desire to give back and to carry the message, our spirit and our Fellowship both benefit.

We are the ones who make NA happen. Our service centers may employ special workers, but there are no professional recovering addicts. A member shared, "I get asked to take leadership positions a lot, because I have more cleantime than most people in the room. I have to think carefully about that—whether it's wise, whether I should step aside and let someone else have a chance, or whether my experience is really needed. I can only get to the right answer if I keep my ego in check."

We must take care not to treat any one member as if they were more or less important than another. This can be even more of a challenge than the struggles we have with those of whom we are naturally suspicious. When we allow our more charismatic members to get away with something, we harm them as much as ourselves. We set ourselves up for conflict and disunity. Acting in ways that lack integrity can become habitual: When we get away with it for a while, we start to forget that what we are doing is wrong. When it starts feeling "normal" for some members to have prestige or for the rules to apply only sometimes, we are not respecting the spirit of anonymity. The idea that we place principles before personalities means that NA service must never be a popularity contest.

Our relationships in service reflect the relationships in our lives. We can come to these relationships in a spirit of harmony and love, or from a place of suspicion and fear. Trusting each other doesn't mean that we reject accountability; we put routines in place to protect ourselves, and our trusted servants, from the types of mistakes we, as addicts, are liable to make. Active trust involves helping each other bring our best to the process. When we serve together in a spirit of love, we remember why we are all here.

Differences of opinion that threaten to tear us apart begin to shrink to proper proportion when we focus on our primary purpose. Our task in Step Twelve is to help each other in a spirit of anonymity. Regardless of our personal differences, we help save each other's lives. This can be particularly challenging when we have personal history that has given us good reasons to dislike or distrust each other. The trust this Tradition asks us to practice is not blind. Especially after we have been here a while, we know what kinds of defects addicts tend to act out on, and we know the people we serve with. Placing principles before personalities is easier said than done. In service, we persist in tolerance, forgiveness, and hope. We find the courage to address sensitive matters—which may bring an emotional reaction from other members—and the wisdom to exercise compassion when doing so. We allow each other to recover in dignity and to serve with selflessness, because we know a Power greater than ourselves is present in the process. This exercise in anonymity will continue to challenge us throughout our recovery.

Personalities themselves don't conflict with principles, but sometimes our actions do. We may have to check ourselves: Is this person actually out of line, or are we just frustrated by who they are? Is this member really the best one for the role, or are we voting for them because they are our friend, or because we want them to like us? Are we responding to their actions or their personalities? Are we asking some members to adhere more closely to guidelines than others? If an action is wrong, it's wrong no matter who is doing it. If an action is right, it deserves our support no matter who is doing it. Walking that walk is what it means to have integrity.

Serving in a spirit of anonymity can be amazingly freeing. We are able to focus on what is being said, not who is speaking. Listening is an essential part of service, and many of us learn these skills for the first time when we serve as secretary or chairperson. We can help a member with whom we disagree find the words to make their point. Our willingness to hear each other and help each other in service in this way reaffirms our understanding that we aren't out to gain anything from another's recovery except gratitude in seeing each other recover. We get to feel that "quiet satisfaction in being useful," as one of our Basic Text stories says.

We learn to trust the process. Of course, trust doesn't always come easily. A member shared, "I have to let go and trust that, while they may not be doing the task the way I would do it, it's getting done and it will be all right. Their way might be good too. Their way might even be better!" If we stick around long enough, we sometimes get to see the ideas we opposed actually work out for the best—because they were right, or because we learned through the experience. And we see our ideas and contributions make a difference in shaping NA. It may take a long view to see the fruits of our labor. We don't give up, whether it's five minutes or ten years before the miracle happens.

We come together in unity not in spite of our differences, but with great pleasure in them. We have such a wide variety of experience and perspective to share with each other and to help us carry our message. Service in NA is anonymity in action. We act in a spirit of equality and goodwill, setting none of us above others. We celebrate each other's successes, even when we have disagreed profoundly. We serve not for recognition or approval but to help carry our message to the addict who suffers. When we serve in a spirit of anonymity we remember that our unity must come first, and that the powerful relationship between the First Tradition and the Twelfth holds us together, even when we feel like we will surely come apart.

The power of Tradition Twelve in our service allows us to bear witness to greatness, to find joy and comfort in work, and to participate in making Narcotics Anonymous. A just-for-today program is always beginning anew. Each of us is founding NA, today, right where we are. Each of us is building hope for ourselves and for the addict yet to come. We know that the work we do in service has effects far past our ability to see or imagine. Allowing ourselves to be part of this work is a gift to ourselves even more than to those we serve.

WORKSHOP QUESTIONS _____

The questions below offer a way to begin—or continue—a service discussion or workshop focused on this Tradition.

1. Why is anonymity so important in service? How does practicing this principle change how we approach our service efforts?

2. Does our approach to service change when we allow those we serve to have anonymity? When we allow it for those with whom we serve? When we apply it to ourselves? How do our service efforts together change when each of us practices this Tradition?

3. Discuss the connection between unity and anonymity. How does our practice of anonymity support unity? Can we experience unity without anonymity? When we practice anonymity and unity together, what about our service efforts changes?

4. What part does anonymity play in our selection of trusted servants? How can we consider qualifications, requirements, and skills without making it personal?

5. Do we hold some members to a higher standard than others? Do we excuse behavior in some that we do not tolerate from others?

6. What can we do to be more inclusive in our service efforts? How can we attract and retain members in service? How do we balance our need for continuity with the practice of rotation?

7. Do we treat more experienced trusted servants as if they have greater authority or importance than those who are newer to the work? Do our efforts at consensus offer equal respect and importance to everyone's input?

8. How does this Tradition help us understand anonymity? How does anonymity help us understand this Tradition? How do we practice anonymity in terms of this Tradition?

9. Discuss any bridges between this Tradition and one or more of the Twelve Concepts. What do these bridges teach us about our service efforts?

10. What more can we do to bring the principles of this Tradition into our service efforts? What could we do differently to better carry out our services?

Our Traditions as a whole are about learning to love. We learn to live in peace and dignity with others, to take care of ourselves as we reach out to help, to offer a hand without overstepping or demanding anything in return. Our concern for others is no longer based in what they can do for us, or even whether or how much we like them. We care because we share a common problem and a common solution, and in that we find common ground and common purpose.

Anonymity offers us spiritual safety, an ability to see the work of a Power greater than ourselves all around us. We begin to trust that force as a presence for goodness in our own lives. We learn to take risks, trust, share, and care. Anonymity is not the natural state of an addict, although many addicts die nameless and alone. Anonymity opens our heart to the addict who is suffering whether that person is known or unknown to us, whether we have reason to trust or mistrust, whether we are afraid or alone or busy or we are ready to reach out, right now, today. When we reach out a loving hand in a spirit of anonymity and faith, a Power greater than ourselves is at work. In anonymity, we are free to be ourselves and to carry and receive a message of hope with the addict who suffers, regardless of whenever, wherever, or whoever they might be.

ALL WILL BE WELL

"They are truly the ties that bind us together.
It is only through understanding and
application that they work."

There are many ways to approach our Traditions. We study and practice them differently around the world and around the neighborhood. It seems like a paradox to say at once that they are not negotiable and that we practice them differently—but it's that simple. Our principles are the same. They are universal because they are true, and they work. Whether we write about these principles, discuss them with other members, or simply practice them in our groups, each of us comes to an understanding for ourselves. The principles do not change, but as we grow and mature in recovery, as the base of our personal experience widens, our understandings of the Traditions deepen. When we come together in unity and goodwill, we weave our varied experience and understanding into a single, clear voice. A group finds its conscience not through uniformity, but by coming to a shared understanding and putting that into action.

None of our Traditions stands alone. We cannot practice some and not others. We do best when we don't try to "enforce" one Tradition or another, at the expense of unity or at the expense of another addict's right to membership. Instead, we share perspectives and lessons and trust our fellows to follow their conscience as we follow ours. Carrying our message can be a life-and-death proposition for us, and a loving Higher Power is our ultimate authority. Each of us has the choice to be a member of Narcotics Anonymous, and all members are equal. When we practice the Twelve Traditions, we are creating a Fellowship that takes its guidance from spiritual principles rather than individual personalities.

In our NA groups, the Traditions guide us to create an atmosphere of recovery in which we can find the identification and empathy we so desperately need. In service, the Traditions keep us on course. They guide us to work together in a spirit of unity and interact with those around us in ways that are appropriate and productive. The Traditions teach us as individuals what it means to be members of a Fellowship, and how to live within our NA communities. We also learn more about who we are in relation to family, community, work, and intimacy. The principles we learn in the Traditions become part of what we practice in all our affairs. They bring peace in our hearts and unity in our lives.

The spirit of service is a blend of passion and compassion. Addicts are remarkable, resourceful, and creative. When we get excited about something, there's no telling how far we can go with it. The Twelve Traditions guide us to moderate our enthusiasm with clarity about what matters to us and the wisdom of experience. When we know our purpose, our work can be focused. When we can see the pitfalls awaiting us, we can take action to avoid them before we stumble. Our Traditions show us our purpose, our path, and the obstacles in our way. We go forward with optimism and caution, with joy and hope. We learn from our own experience and from the experience of those who have gone before us. Willingness fuels our action; open-mindedness allows us to learn from experience and to bring imagination and creativity to our service without losing sight of our principles.

Recovery didn't begin for us when we wished for it; it began when we heard a message and started taking action to save our lives. We can't take creative action if we are afraid to take a risk. In service, in our lives, in our relationships, we apply the principles of recovery to the best of our ability. Even when we try our best, we will sometimes make mistakes. In these moments, it can help to remember that we are in the care of a loving Higher Power. We learn in our personal struggles that recovery is strong enough to withstand the storms of life. We learn through service that the NA program is strong enough to hold us all, and our principles are more powerful than our worst ideas. We work together to face the challenges that arise in service and also to solve the problems that we create. When we take on the task in a spirit of love, unity, and compassion, we turn painful learning moments into opportunities for forgiveness, growth, and transformation.

Creative action keeps us moving forward. Anonymity in action keeps us out of our own way, ensuring that our principles always come before our personalities. Our principles are primary, just as our purpose is primary. Anonymity in action describes how we act. What we do is up to us, as long as we are moving in the right direction—toward our primary purpose, focused on the addicts who still suffer.

The Traditions serve to define the first word of the First Step: "We." Suffering addicts, hopeless and desperate, have come together and built a Fellowship that is saving lives around the world. NA wasn't created by a bunch of well-meaning observers, and in each new place where NA grows, addicts in that community get clean, find a new way of life, and carry the message to still-suffering addicts. The process is the same from Brazil to Brussels, from Kentucky to Kenya, from Sydney to Seoul. Our Traditions tell the story and offer the tools to help us do that same thing over and over: stop using drugs, lose the desire to use, find a new way to live. And go help another addict.

Each of us, every day, is creating Narcotics Anonymous. Each new day, we are beginning. And the process of serving selflessly, carrying the message, building our Fellowship, "growing our we"—that process heals our hearts and lifts our spirits. Every addict in Narcotics Anonymous expands the possibility of freedom for every other addict in Narcotics Anonymous. Sometimes we know who saves our lives; often we have no idea what chain of events leads to us hearing what we need when we need it. Our collective wisdom grows every day. Our Traditions teach us how to take that wisdom—our shared experience, strength, and hope—and apply it to help ourselves and our fellow addicts, today and every day.

Like a lighthouse on the rocky shore, guiding us away from danger, the Twelve Traditions of Narcotics Anonymous help us navigate in accordance with our principles, our purpose, and our paths. This is not the final word on our Traditions, but the beginning of a journey with the principles as our guide. So long as we follow this way, all will be well.

TWELVE STEPS OF NARCOTICS ANONYMOUS

1. We admitted that we were powerless over our addiction, that our lives had become unmanageable.

2. We came to believe that a Power greater than ourselves could restore us to sanity.

3. We made a decision to turn our will and our lives over to the care of God *as we understood Him.*

4. We made a searching and fearless moral inventory of ourselves.

5. We admitted to God, to ourselves, and to another human being the exact nature of our wrongs.

6. We were entirely ready to have God remove all these defects of character.

7. We humbly asked Him to remove our shortcomings.

8. We made a list of all persons we had harmed, and became willing to make amends to them all.

9. We made direct amends to such people wherever possible, except when to do so would injure them or others.

10. We continued to take personal inventory and when we were wrong promptly admitted it.

11. We sought through prayer and meditation to improve our conscious contact with God *as we understood Him*, praying only for knowledge of His will for us and the power to carry that out.

12. Having had a spiritual awakening as a result of these steps, we tried to carry this message to addicts, and to practice these principles in all our affairs.

TWELVE TRADITIONS OF NARCOTICS ANONYMOUS

1. Our common welfare should come first; personal recovery depends on NA unity.

2. For our group purpose there is but one ultimate authority—a loving God as He may express Himself in our group conscience. Our leaders are but trusted servants; they do not govern.

3. The only requirement for membership is a desire to stop using.

4. Each group should be autonomous except in matters affecting other groups or NA as a whole.

5. Each group has but one primary purpose—to carry the message to the addict who still suffers.

6. An NA group ought never endorse, finance, or lend the NA name to any related facility or outside enterprise, lest problems of money, property or prestige divert us from our primary purpose.

7. Every NA group ought to be fully self-supporting, declining outside contributions.

8. Narcotics Anonymous should remain forever nonprofessional, but our service centers may employ special workers.

9. NA, as such, ought never be organized, but we may create service boards or committees directly responsible to those they serve.

10. Narcotics Anonymous has no opinion on outside issues; hence the NA name ought never be drawn into public controversy.

11. Our public relations policy is based on attraction rather than promotion; we need always maintain personal anonymity at the level of press, radio, and films.

12. Anonymity is the spiritual foundation of all our Traditions, ever reminding us to place principles before personalities.

TWELVE CONCEPTS
FOR NA SERVICE

1. To fulfill our fellowship's primary purpose, the NA groups have joined together to create a structure which develops, coordinates, and maintains services on behalf of NA as a whole.

2. The final responsibility and authority for NA services rests with the NA groups.

3. The NA groups delegate to the service structure the authority necessary to fulfill the responsibilities assigned to it.

4. Effective leadership is highly valued in Narcotics Anonymous. Leadership qualities should be carefully considered when selecting trusted servants.

5. For each responsibility assigned to the service structure, a single point of decision and accountability should be clearly defined.

6. Group conscience is the spiritual means by which we invite a loving God to influence our decisions.

7. All members of a service body bear substantial responsibility for that body's decisions and should be allowed to fully participate in its decision-making processes.

8. Our service structure depends on the integrity and effectiveness of our communications.

9. All elements of our service structure have the responsibility to carefully consider all viewpoints in their decision-making processes.

10. Any member of a service body can petition that body for the redress of a personal grievance, without fear of reprisal.

11. NA funds are to be used to further our primary purpose, and must be managed responsibly.

12. In keeping with the spiritual nature of Narcotics Anonymous, our structure should always be one of service, never of government.

A VISION FOR NA SERVICE

All of the efforts of Narcotics Anonymous are inspired by the primary purpose of our groups. Upon this common ground we stand committed.

Our vision is that one day:

- Every addict in the world has the chance to experience our message in his or her own language and culture and find the opportunity for a new way of life;

- Every member, inspired by the gift of recovery, experiences spiritual growth and fulfillment through service;

- NA service bodies worldwide work together in a spirit of unity and cooperation to support the groups in carrying our message of recovery;

- Narcotics Anonymous has universal recognition and respect as a viable program of recovery.

Honesty, trust, and goodwill are the foundation of our service efforts, all of which rely upon the guidance of a loving Higher Power.